TOTAL
Investing

TOTAL Investing

THOMAS J. HOLT

ARLINGTON HOUSE · PUBLISHERS
NEW ROCHELLE, NEW YORK

Library of Congress Catalog Card Number HG4521.H73 332.6′7
75–33906
ISBN 0–87000–357–7

Manufactured in the United States of America

Library of Congress Cataloging in Publication Data

Holt, Thomas J 1928–
Total investing.

1. Investments. I. Title.
HG4521.H73 332.6′7 75–33906
ISBN 0–87000–357–7

To my wife Debbie

CONTENTS

TOTAL Investing

CHAPTER 1

You Don't Need a Bull Market to Make Money

INTERIM RISES notwithstanding, the stock market has been a disaster area in the last several years for most investors. Literally hundreds of billions of dollars have been erased from their net worth. Had the losses been suffered only by the uninformed, it wouldn't have been so bad. Wall Street has always warned that the public should seek professional guidance from stock brokers and other investment experts.

But the pros are the ones that have failed. Securities recommended in recent years by those armies of "chartered financial analysts" have brought untold millions of dollars of losses to trusting customers. Investors who have relied on mutual funds have fared little better. Even the supposedly low-risk balanced funds are now worth but a fraction of the lofty prices paid in the late 1960's by unsuspecting investors.

For a little while, at least the money managers at the big banks looked good. By zeroing in the tens of billions they controlled on a handful of favorite issues, they were able to manufacture excellent performance records. But in 1973 and 1974, the free-market selling pressure was far too strong even for them to overcome;

their darling issues plummetted. So staggering were the losses sustained by the trusts and pension funds they managed that in less than two years, virtually all the preceding decade's growth was erased.

Almost to a man, security analysts and money managers blamed their failure on the bear market. True, stock prices are no longer being pushed onward and upward by an ever-roaring bull market. But even quack doctors have enough pride not to blame their own shortcomings on their patients' lack of good health. Investment, it appears, is a "profession" in which experts are dependable only when circumstances are absolutely favorable to them.

But not all professionals are bull-market heroes. Some can indeed help investors protect and build capital in any kind of market. The company I head has done just that for most clients.

Let me show you our track record*. In doing so, I am obviously bragging. But please bear with me. Having worked hard for this record, I am, of course, proud of it. For this book to be useful to you, I must first establish credibility. Investors have become very skeptical of investment experts these days—and justifiably so. To prove my point—that you, too, don't need a bull market to make money—I think I'd better back it up with hard facts and figures.

Until we introduced in 1975 an asset management service for institutions and an option-selecting publication for traders, T. J. Holt & Company had been offering three investment services. The youngest may be the most relevant to our discussion because it has never known a "good" market; it was launched on May 1, 1973, when the Dow Jones industrial average stood well over 900. *The Aggressive Trading Portfolio* is a service designed for a limited number of well-to-do investors interested in playing the "beat the market" game. Participants receive, at irregular intervals, specific recommendations as to what, how and when to buy or sell.

To monitor the program, we set up a Model Portfolio to re-

*The updated records of the three services discussed herein are available to anyone upon request from T. J. Holt & Company, Inc. 277 Park Ave., New York, N. Y. 10017.

THE HOLT 500 AGGRESSIVE TRADING PORTFOLIO
(Model Portfolio vs. Standard & Poor's Composite Index)

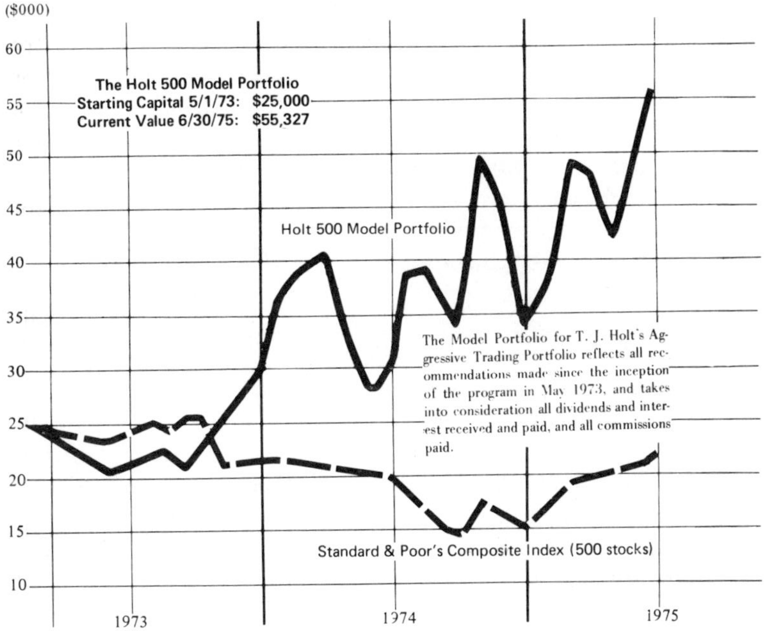

This Model Portfolio demonstrates the actual progress of The Holt 500 Aggressive Trading Portfolio since its inception in May 1973 with an initial capital of $25,000 (adjusted for a subsequent 2-for-1 split). As such, it reflects all recommendations made, and is based on the opening price of the individual security on the day following the date of recommendation. The computation takes into consideration commissions, transfer taxes and interest paid as well as dividends and interest earned.

Individual subscribers to this Holt service are at liberty to tailor their trading portfolio to their specific needs and resources. Therefore, this Model Portfolio cannot be taken as representative of actual results obtained by individual subscribers, nor does it imply in any way that all Holt 500 Aggressive Trading Portfolio participants have achieved like results. The extent to which individuals have recorded results on a par with the Model Portfolio depends upon when their participation began, how faithfully they have followed Holt's recommendations, the price at which they executed particular advices and their allocation of funds to specific securities. In all probability, some have fared better, some worse.

There's no assurance that The Aggressive Trading Portfolio will perform profitably in the future, or that it will perform as well in the future as in the past.

flect the very same trades recommended to clients and using the same prices that clients were able to get. That portfolio originally had a starting capital of $25,000, adjusted for a 2-for-1 split put into effect in late 1974. At the end of June 1975, a little more than two years later, it had a market value of $55,327, even after allowing for all commissions and other related expenses. That's a 121.3% gain. During that same 26-month period, the popular averages had shown a loss.

To be sure, two years is not a very long time to evaluate any market performance conclusively. All too often, Wall Street experts run "hot" for a year or two, only to fall flat on their faces thereafter. Moreover, the Aggressive Trading Portfolio program is designed only for those who can afford to speculate; it trades in and out quite frequently and uses margin extensively. In these difficult times, the average investor really should not engage in such a high-risk, high-stake game.

Strategic Money Management, our second service, may therefore be more indicative of our *investment* record. Introduced in 1971, this service manages individual and corporate portfolios on a discretionary basis.

Strategic Money Management accounts are handled individually. Hence there is no such thing as an average account. We have done very well for some clients but not so well for others. Thus, even if we could compute an average performance record for diverse accounts having different starting dates, different personal backgrounds and different investment goals, it would be misleading. It would be similarly misleading to give you the results for our best accounts—or, for that matter, for our worst accounts.

We do have available, however, a Showcase Portfolio designed to show how a Strategic Money Management account seeking growth primarily might have performed. This hypothetical account is maintained at the Special Management Service Department of Dean Witter & Co., in Los Angeles, California. It started with $100,000 on December 15, 1971. By the end of June 1975, it had a market value of $307,397—a gain of 207.4% in three and a half years.

For those who think that even three and a half years is not long

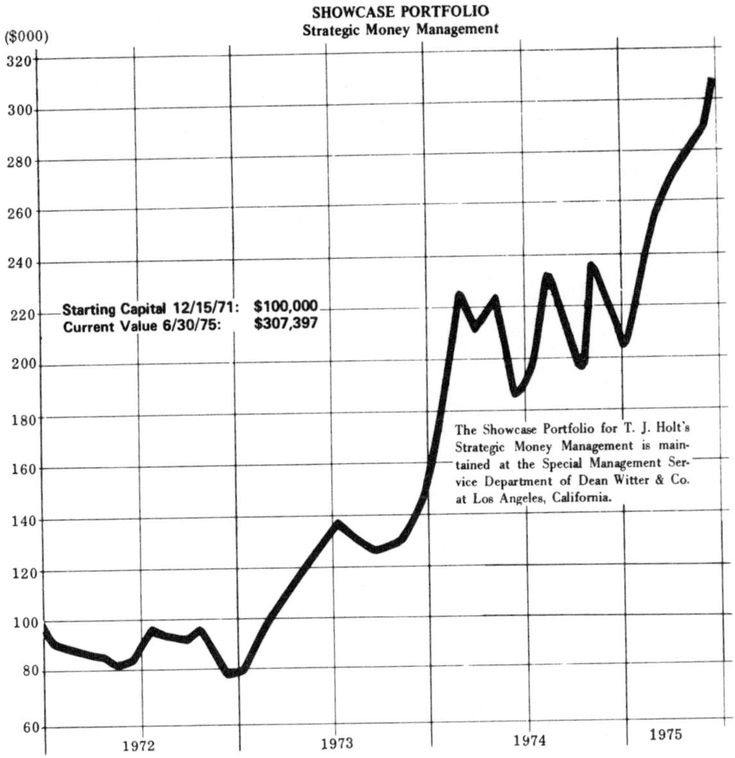

T. J. Holt & Company's Showcase Portfolio is designed to illustrate how a Strategic Money Management account seeking primarily growth and willing to accept businessmen's risks might have performed. Buy, sell and short sale orders for this hypothetical account are placed with Dean Witter & Co. in the same manner as those for clients' accounts. The tabulation does not include dividends and interest paid or received, nor management fee; but it does reflect all normal commission charges and transfer taxes.

This presentation does not imply in any way that all Strategic Money Management accounts have performed equally well. No actual account, in fact, is an exact duplication of this portfolio. Some clients have done better, some worse.

There's no assurance that Strategic Money Management in general and this Showcase Portfolio in particular will perform as well in the future as in the past, or that they will be profitable.

enough to judge investment results, let me offer the complete performance record of *The Holt Investment Advisory.*

We began publishing this service in early May 1967. From the very start, it has followed a firm policy of putting on record every specific recommendation made. It also regularly provides investors with "round trip" advice. For every buy recommendation, there is a subsequent sell recommendation; and vice versa. Until the close-out advice is given, every recommended security remains on an Open Recommendation list and regular follow-ups are published.

July 1, 1975

THE HOLT INVESTMENT ADVISORY

277 PARK AVENUE, NEW YORK, NEW YORK 10017

COMPLETE PERFORMANCE RECORD
OF HOLT'S SECURITIES RECOMMENDATIONS
50 Open Recommendations (Page 1)

SECURITY	BUY (SHORT) RECOMMENDATION Issue Date	Price	DJIA	6/30/75 CLOSING (DJIA - 879)	NO. OF MONTHS HELD	% CHANGE Stock	DJIA
ASA Ltd.	11/24/67	11 1/4*	874	45 1/2	91	+304.4	+ 0.6
Welkom Gold Mining (ADR)	3/15/68	5 1/4	842	6 3/8	87½	+ 21.4	+ 4.4
Hecla Mining	10/17/69	25.85*	830	23 1/2	68½	- 9.1	+ 5.9
Western Deep Levels (ADR)	1/9/70	9 1/4	802	28 3/4	66	+210.8	+ 9.6
International Mining	9/18/70	12 3/8	754	10 5/8	57½	- 14.1	+16.6
Sunshine Mining 6½s, '89	4/16/71	101	933	105 1/8	50½	+ 4.1	- 5.8
Kloof Gold (ADR)	10/15/71	6	889	15 3/4	44½	+162.5	- 1.1
St. Helena Gold (ADR)	10/15/71	11 1/4	889	42 1/4	44½	+275.6	- 1.1
Fairchild Industries 4 3/8s, 1992	1/21/72	66	915	49 1/8	41½	- 25.6	- 3.9
Grumman 4¼s, 1992	1/21/72	63	915	56 5/8	41½	- 10.1	- 3.9
Lockheed 4¼s, 1992	1/21/72	46 1/2	915	41 1/2	41½	- 10.8	- 3.9

July 1, 1975

COMPLETE PERFORMANCE RECORD
OF HOLT'S SECURITIES RECOMMENDATIONS
191 Closed Out Recommendations (Page 1)

page 3

SECURITY	BUY (SHORT) RECOMMENDATION Issue Date	Price	DJIA	SELL OR COVER RECOMMENDATION Issue Date	Price	DJIA	NO. OF MONTHS HELD	% CHANGE Stock	DJIA
Archer Daniels Midland	6/2/67	46	853	12/1/67	57	883	6	+ 23.9	+ 3.5
Hilton Hotels	6/2/67	33	853	12/1/67	62	883	6	+ 87.9	+ 3.5
Kewanee Oil	5/5/67	23	897	12/1/67	34	883	7	+ 47.8	- 1.6
Pan American Sulphur	5/5/67	21	897	12/1/67	38	883	7	+ 81.0	- 1.6
Sheraton Corp.	6/2/67	15	853	12/1/67	30	883	6	+100.0	+ 3.5
Benrus Watch	6/16/67	11	881	2/1/68	15 1/2	855	7½	+ 40.9	- 3.0
Du Pont	5/19/67	162	882	2/1/68	156	855	6½	- 3.7	- 3.1
General American Oil	5/5/67	35	897	3/1/68	42	845	10	+ 20.0	- 5.8
Interpace	10/6/67	23	921	7/5/68	31	897	9	+ 34.8	- 2.6
U.S. Pipe and Foundry	10/6/67	25	921	7/5/68	29	897	9	+ 16.0	- 2.6
Financial Federation	9/1/67	21	894	12/6/68	36	985	15	+ 71.4	+10.2
Great Western Financial	9/1/67	17	894	12/6/68	28	985	15	+ 64.7	+10.2

July 1, 1975

COMPLETE PERFORMANCE RECORD
OF HOLT'S SECURITIES RECOMMENDATIONS

page 7

Summary of All Recommendations

Average change for all 241 recommendations (50 open + 191 closed out	+25.49%	+1.57%
Average holding period	16.5 months	
Average annualized change	+18.51%	+1.14%

It should not be assumed that recommendations made in the future will be profitable or will equal the performance of prior recommendations.

This performance record does not include dividends, interest, commissions and taxes.

The Dow-Jones industrial average is used for comparison only because it is the most readily available and popularly watched reference to indicate the general market trend for corresponding time periods. Performance records, however, cannot be measured by direct comparison with the DJIA since the latter comprises 30 seasoned blue chips. Those 30 have performed better than both the market and mutual funds in recent years.

Moreover, while the DJIA is "fully invested" at all times, the Advisory recommends a flexible portfolio composition, periodically adjusting the proportion of funds allocated to stocks, ADR's, bonds, convertibles, warrants, hedges, and in a bear market, short sales. This performance record of the Advisory's specific securities recommendations does not reflect the Advisory's advice on market strategy.

As of the end of June 1975, The Holt Investment Advisory had made 241 security recommendations altogether. Of that total, 50 were still open, while 191 had been closed out. On average, those 241 recommendations had appreciated 25.5% as against a 1.6% gain for the Dow Jones industrial average over the same time. The average holding period was 16.5 months, or a little less than one and a half years.

Annualized, the Holt recommendations scored an average gain of 18.5%, versus 1.1% for the Dow Jones industrial average. Note that an annual growth of 18.5%, when compounded, comes to over 445% in ten years. (These calculations do not include dividends, interest or commissions. Had they been included, the total return would be a few percentage points higher still.)

In presenting the specific percentage gains achieved by our three services, I am not suggesting by any means that we can always do that well for our clients in the future. As a matter of fact, those performance figures change from month to month—sometimes higher, sometimes lower. Besides, no investor can possibly act on every single recommendation made by the Advisory. The actual results attained by individual subscribers may thus differ widely from our records.

But I hope the track record of our firm, spanning as it does more than eight years of both good and bad markets, has helped me convince you that the conventional Wall Street wisdom has let the public down unnecessarily in recent years. Capital can indeed by built without the help of a roaring bull market.

CHAPTER 2

The Winning Combination

WHY HAS OUR FIRM been able to achieve such results in a period when most investors were hit with heavy losses? Maybe Lady Luck has been kind to us. But again with due humility, I think you'll agree that no investor can be lucky, or right for the wrong reason, for so many years—unless there is a roaring bull market to help forgive investment sins. I submit, therefore, that our achievement is attributable mainly to our willingness to be flexible and to our insistence on using common sense.

Let me emphasize right at this point that I am not suggesting that by being flexible and by using common sense, anyone—including myself—can guarantee profits in the future. Investing always involves some risk, and as long as there is risk, there is the danger of loss.

Moreover, to invest successfully, flexibility and common sense must be supplemented by good independent research. Only with solid knowledge can the investor maintain unyielding faith in his decision. And only with conviction can he overcome mass psychology and avoid emotional strain. So this book will not offer any simple, magic formula for getting rich overnight.

Nevertheless, as you read this book, you will probably discover that my basic concept is easy to understand and, more importantly, that it is logical. And I believe you will also agree that in the long run, a flexible investment approach based on cool-headed common sense is bound to be far more effective than buying stocks haphazardly or emotionally. Common-sense investing is based on facts and logic. It is guided by what the economic and market environment *is,* not by what we would like it to be.

Specifically, I put investment flexibility and common sense to work via the Total Investment Approach. What is the Total Investment Approach? Let me put it this way. When practicing the Total Investment Approach, an investor must:

1) be willing and able to analyze economic and market developments independently;

2) be prepared to adjust investment strategies quickly as economic and market conditions change, shifting portfolio composition to reduce risk exposure as well as to take advantage of free-market forces;

3) be open-minded enough to recognize, and make use of, investment opportunities offered by securities and techniques other than buying common stocks; and

4) be ready to take a minority position steadfastly, whenever necessary.

In short, it is an approach unencumbered by rigid, conventional Wall Street thinking.

Now doesn't that make sense? When the market is trending downward, obviously you should minimize the equity holdings in your portfolio, investing instead in other securities like bonds or Treasury bills. Conversely, when stocks are expected to advance broadly, you should take full advantage of it by investing heavily in equities, or even in such high-leverage securities as warrants and call options.

Simple though this approach may sound, it is a fact that most people think of investing only in terms of common stocks. They automatically take for granted that fixed-income securities are too stuffy, or that warrants and call options are too risky. Moreover, most investors either put all their investment capital in stocks or pull out of the market altogether. Seldom do they consider investing just a portion of their capital in equities and allocating the rest to other investment vehicles.

Finally, many investors refuse to pay attention to economic developments or the underlying market trend. "Just tell me which stock to buy," they say. "Don't bother me with economics." Others ask, "Why worry about the economy? The market has already discounted whatever is in prospect. Besides, most economists are wrong anyway."

But individual stocks do not exist in a vacuum. Their performances are very much influenced by economic and market factors, as well as company developments. Without a good understanding of the overall economy and market environment, no one can truly feel comfortable with his holdings and take advantage of mass myopia with conviction.

It's true that most economists are wrong, especially around major turning points. It's also true that the market often discounts many months in advance what "informed" investors anticipate for the economy. But that's precisely why it's important to include in the Total Investment Approach a good knowledge of economic and monetary prospects. *Profit opportunities in the securities market are most abundant and the risks involved are lowest when the "sophisticated" have misinterpreted current developments and when stocks and bonds have discounted the wrong prospect.*

It's hard for the lay investor to analyze the economy or to foresee the market trend correctly. With the so-called standard forecast usually wrong, it's difficult for him to anticipate market fluctuations by changing investment strategy. But that can be remedied by getting the right information from the right source and doing the right kind of homework. Later in this book, I will explain how common sense, along with the Flow-of-Funds analysis, can help in this respect.

Even without analytical foresight, however, there are often times when investors instinctively realize that the market is headed downward. During the early 1970's, for instance, polls repeatedly indicated that the public was becoming pessimistic over the economy and was turning sour on the stock market. Yet the typical investor hung on to his sinking holdings in the hope that somehow his particular stocks would be spared in the stormy market. This is a clear example of investors letting personal emotion overcome logic.

Actually, the ability to adjust equity positions speedily puts the individual investor one up on the big institutions. The collapse of the glamour stocks in 1974 illustrated the immobility of such overweight investors as pension funds managed by the big banks. The money managers simply could not unload their concentrated holdings in any significant amounts without immediately deflating the market prices of the issues involved.

The individual investor, on the other hand, is far less muscle-bound, faster on his feet. Even the wealthy can usually liquidate all equity positions in their multimillion-dollar portfolios in a matter of days without significantly damaging the value of their holdings.

Remember, in a free-market system, everyone—investor as well as businessman—should make full use of whatever special ability he has to outperform his competitors.

To utilize investment vehicles other than common stocks from time to time is also just a matter of being realistic. When a business contraction is approaching, for instance, common sense would indicate that demand for money would sooner or later soften and that interest rates would ease. Since declining interest rates mean advancing bond prices, switching from stocks to bonds would not only help to protect capital, but would actually enhance the capital growth potential. Yet again, the great majority of investors ignore bonds and think only in terms of buying or selling equities.

To a great extent, Wall Street is responsible for this overemphasis on equities. For most brokers, the chief source of income is commissions generated by securities transactions. Since stock transactions generate much higher commissions than the same amount of money transacted in fixed income securities, many account executives, at least until recently, poohpoohed the latter.

But the successful investor is never a tool of his broker. The fact is, as you will see in this book, it is much easier to understand bonds than to evaluate stocks. And with yields from non-equity issues so generous these days, every investor owes it to himself to at least become familiar with them.

Bonds and debentures by no means complete the list of securities that investors should consider along with common stocks. Warrants and options are just a few other examples. These issues normally involve high leverage; investing in them entails unusual risk. But their judicious use by the astute investor at the right time can also generate big returns. I will discuss them in more detail later.

Some of you may be wondering why my Total Investment Approach does not include buying real estate, gold and silver coins, diamonds and rare art objects, but instead deals only with securities. The answer is simply that buying real estate and valuables does not constitute an efficient use of capital at present.

There's nothing wrong in buying these things if you enjoy holding them. And if you are convinced that inflation will go on and on, it might even be advisable to put some money in such properties as a hedge. But be absolutely clear in your own mind that you're buying those things strictly as an inflation hedge. Don't mislead yourself into believing that you're investing in them.

As I see it, putting money into something that does not produce income or have the potential of generating income in the future is not investing. It is speculating. The owner of such an asset—be it raw land or gold bullion—does not earn any current return on his invested capital. He merely hopes that someday someone will somehow buy it from him at a higher price. In a sense, this is what the so-called "bigger fool" theory is all about.

The trouble with playing this "bigger fool" game, though, is that someone must eventually become the biggest fool of them all. There will be no buyers left who are willing to pay higher prices. If for any reason he has to sell that asset to invest in something that produces income or just to raise cash, that last holder will have to accept lower bids. Nowadays, the danger of becoming that biggest fool is especially great. The desire both for current income and for liquidity (i.e., ready cash) is rising.

Prudent investing, therefore, must involve assets that provide current or potential income. Potential income, because the stock of a company that doesn't pay any dividends currently could be a good investment if that company can reasonably be expected to pay large enough dividends in the foreseeable future to justify the current price.

Similarly, while warrants and options do not provide current income, they are potentially convertible into the related common stocks. Their price performance is therefore directly influenced by that of the equity issues.

When you invest in an income-producing security, the present and potential yields, along with capital market conditions, provide the only reliable basis on which to determine its underlying value. If the income it produces rises, or if interest rates from competing investing vehicles decline, or both, the intrinsic value of that security automatically increases. You won't need a "bigger fool" to take it off your hands. Indeed, if someone offers you a higher price for that investment, it's only because he is *wise* enough to recognize its increased value.

There are, of course, investment vehicles other than securities that produce current income. For example, you can buy an apartment building and collect rent from your tenants; or you can buy a working interest in a producing oil well and receive production income. But none of these investments provide you with the kind of liquidity offered by actively traded securities. And as I mentioned earlier, liquidity is of paramount importance these days.

So you see, there is really nothing mysterious about the Total Investment Approach. It is the flexible approach, the realistic approach, the common-sense approach. And it stresses mobility and liquidity.

If you are willing to forego the conventional Wall Street wisdom, do some homework, and enlarge your investment horizon, I am convinced your investment results will be far more gratifying than they would otherwise be, whether the market turns bullish or bearish.

And, I might add, besides protecting and building capital successfully, you will find unusual satisfaction in being able to outperform the "best minds" of Wall Street.

CHAPTER 3

What Makes Stock Prices Tick, Anyway?

THE HUMAN MIND is like a computer. It processes incoming data along with previously stored information to arrive at an answer. But no matter how sophisticated a computer system is, programmers always say GIGO—garbage in, garbage out. That's why in the last two years those fancy computerized economic models run by major banks, colleges and research foundations have performed just as miserably as human experts. They all failed to anticipate the 1974-75 economic slump—the sharpest business contraction since the Great Depression.

Before adopting my Total Investment Approach, therefore, it will be necessary for you to erase from your mind certain myths and obsolete theories.

Unlike a computer, however, the human mind also thinks and reasons. For any rational person, past knowledge and experience simply cannot be erased or forgotten by just pressing a button. They will keep returning to influence the thinking process. To remove them, therefore, the reasons why they should be purged must be well understood. I shall therefore first try to explain why many of the commonly accepted ideas about investing are unreliable or at least inadequate.

Ask any investor—individual or professional—what he has been using to decide whether to buy or sell stocks, and his answer will probably be one or more of the following: 1) fundamental research, 2) monetary study, 3) technical analysis, and 4) personal feeling or intuition. Then ask him how his investments have done in the last several years. Chances are, they have resulted in losses. The inescapable conclusion: these investment guides are inadequate, if not unreliable.

Why have all those aids which were so helpful in the past suddenly lost their usefulness in recent years? The answer is that they never were dependable.

In a roaring bull market, virtually all stocks go up. In such an environment, any system or theory for buying stocks really has to be super-terrible not to make money for its users. But as many professors have taken pains to prove, buying shares at random can generate results as good as the averages. Hence, in a long-term advancing market, most investment aids are simply right for the wrong reasons.

Unfortunately, since the late 1960's, there is no longer any sustained bull market to help cover up the inadequacies of these methods or theories.

When you come right down to it, stock prices obviously do not *directly* correspond to fundamental or economic developments, monetary trends, chart formations or personal desires. They respond to only one thing—changes in the demand for and the supply of the shares involved. And those changes are influenced by a great variety of factors, of which economic, monetary, technical and psychological developments are just some of the more important ones. The weight these individual developments have on the changes in the overall supply and demand varies from one period to another. And this is where flexibility and common sense come in.

Nevertheless, it's an unfortunate fact that the great majority of "informed" investors believe that stock prices are *directly* correlated to economic growth and, more specifically, to corporate profits. In a way, this is understandable. Every morning, the financial press typically rationalizes the preceding day's market performance by pointing to some late-breaking business events. And brokers typically base their stock-purchase recommendations on good earnings prospects.

Now, unquestionably there is some relationship between economic developments and stock market prices. It's no coincidence that the longest primary bull market took place at a time when the longest economic expansion also unfolded—the quarter century after the Second World War. And it's no coincidence that the worst bear market, forty-odd years ago, was associated with the steepest economic depression.

But history also shows that almost every major market top took place in the very midst of a business boom. Sometimes the highwater mark was registered just a few months before a recession became apparent; but at other times, stock prices started tumbling long, long before there was any inkling of economic softness.

Perhaps what happened in the last few years is a poignant case in point. Corporate after-tax profits rose 26% in 1973 and an additional 17% in 1974. Reflecting management's belief that the profit gains were real, total dividend payments rose from $27.3 billion in 1972 to $29.6 billion in 1973 and to $32.7 billion in 1974. Yet the great majority of investors who bought stocks in 1972 in anticipation of this 1973-74 profit and dividend growth are now suffering sizable paper losses.

Similarly, from 1937 to 1942, the Dow Jones industrial average dropped some 50%. Yet, in those five years the gross national product climbed more than 75% and corporate profits over 85%. Thus, if anyone was bright enough in 1937 to foresee a near doubling of corporate profits in the ensuing five years and invested in stocks heavily, he would have ended up with heavy losses. Just to break even, he would have had to wait some 13 years.

Here's another example. The 1969-70 market decline was one of the steepest in this generation; in just 12 months, the Dow Jones industrial average tumbled from approximately 975 to 625, a loss of some 35%. And yet the 1970 recession was by far the mildest of all the post-World War II economic corrections.

On the other side of the coin, it's not unusual for stock prices to rise when business conditions are gloomy. The final months of 1974, you may recall, was a period of profound economic pessimism. And in the ensuing months, the U.S. economy did enter the deepest depression since the 1930's. Nevertheless, by the summer of 1975, the Dow Jones Industrials had climbed over 50%, while any number of individual issues appreciated 100% or more.

It has been suggested by some that stock prices generally peak in the midst of a business boom and begin rising in the midst of a recession because they have a way of anticipating approaching business trend reversals. That's why the market is regarded by the National Bureau of Economic Research as a key "leading" economic indicator.

But that doesn't make sense. We all know that economists and businessmen have had a hard time making accurate economic forecasts. Therefore, to suggest that investors, collectively, can do better and can somehow predict business upturns and downturns accurately is to defy logic. Later on in this book, I will explain why the stock market appears to be a good leading indicator of economic cycles. Suffice it to say here that the apparent correlation is a coincidence stemming from the fact that stocks and business activities are both influenced by monetary changes, and that the equity market typically reacts to such changes faster than the economy.

Actually, the stock market has, over the years, discounted quite a number of business reversals prematurely, to say the least. For instance, while the bear market that started in 1937 correctly anticipated the 1937-38 recession, resumption of that bear market in late 1938 anticipated a recession that didn't take place until 1945. True, the advent of World War II helped the economy. But even before Pearl Harbor, stock prices were pointing downward persistently while industrial production was showing one of the sharpest increases on record.

In the spring of 1962, the Dow Jones industrial average tumbled nearly 30% in just three months. The business recession that it "discounted" didn't begin until late 1969, more than $7^1/_2$ years later.

Conversely, from late 1929 to the spring of 1930, the market, as measured by the Dow Jones Industrials, climbed nearly 50% in less than half a year. The "economic recovery" it discounted turned out to be the most devastating depression in this nation's history.

In pointing out all these divergences between the stock market and the economy, I'm not suggesting that economic developments have no bearing on the stock market. As a matter of fact, I consider a down-to-earth analysis of the economic prospect to be a prime prerequisite to successful investing. The purpose of anticipating business trends, however, is to determine how the prospective development will affect the supply of and demand for stocks.

At any one time, whether a rising economy increases the demand for or boosts the supply of stocks depends on many other circumstances. To illustrate, economic expansion normally generates increased corporate and personal savings. As a result, new investment funds are created and some of them may be put into equities. That bolsters the demand. Prosperity also brings about higher corporate earnings and dividends, which in turn attract stock buying by those investors who are normally impressed by such corporate progress.

On the other hand, a booming economy sooner or later requires corporations to expand manufacturing facilities. At some point, increasing capital investments must be financed by heavy outside funds. The resultant offerings of new equity issues represent an increase in the supply of stocks, thereby depressing equity prices. Also, in a period of active business, interest rates typically rise. When the lush interest rates available from fixed-income securities entice shareholders to sell stocks to buy bonds, the active supply of stocks in the open market also increases.

The upshot, then, is that it is important for investors to understand economic developments. But it is also important for them to realize that a growing economy does not automatically mean rising stock prices and vice versa. I will discuss later in this book how to use such information to analyze the market.

CHAPTER 4

Two Wrongs Don't Make a Right

SINCE THE LATE 1960's, the banking system has experienced quite a few credit crunches. In those periods, interest rates in general and short-term rates in particular rose sharply; and stock prices declined. As a result, a growing number of investors as well as analysts have been relying increasingly on monetary analysis as a way to anticipate stock market movements.

These new monetary experts measure changes in the money supply over a variety of time spans. To make sure they don't miss a thing, they subdivide money supply into M1, M2, M3, and so on. Every Thursday afternoon, they watch the news ticker anxiously for the latest weekly Federal Reserve figures on industrial and commercial bank loans and other key banking statistics. Tightening credit and rising interest rates, they have discovered, augur poorly for the stock market.

There is no doubt that, like economic research, keeping abreast of developments in the banking system and in the money and capital market is essential to successful investing. But like economic research, monetary study should not be used blindly.

Actually, it is not true at all that rising interest rates always result in lowering stock prices. We all know, for example, that the longest and strongest bull market in history took place in the quarter century after the second World War. Yet, throughout that period, money and credit were becoming costlier and scarcer. Back in 1945, when the Dow Jones industrials were selling well below 200, short-term interest rates were running below 1% and long-term bond yields stood just a bit over 2%. Interest rates are many times higher at present, of course. But so are stock prices, the recent bear market notwithstanding.

The fact again is, monetary developments are just another one of many factors affecting the supply of and demand for common stocks. Sometimes, a rise in interest rates encourages an increase in equity purchases; other times, it motivates a speedup in the rate of liquidation. Instead of depending on some simple correlation, one must figure out how such developments affect the supply and demand relationship in the specific economic and market environment under study. That's something the new breed of analysts have failed to do.

Whereas "informed" investors typically rely heavily on fundamental economic and monetary research, most private investors pay little attention to such developments. Few of them know how fast the gross national product is growing, what discount rate the Federal Reserve is charging, or how many passenger cars auto dealers are selling. Nor do they care.

More often than not, their decisions to buy or sell stocks are based strictly on their personal feeling. If, for whatever reason, they happen to like a certain company, they buy its stock. The underlying assumption is that the stock of a good company must be a good investment.

In a way, that's fully understandable. To their way of thinking, a corporation that has a good product and an able management is bound to grow. And the only way to participate in that growth is to become a stockholder. True, they reason, the fortune of such a company may be temporarily hurt by a recession, a labor strike, or whatever; but long-term investors shouldn't worry about such things. As long as an enterprising firm grows and grows, an equity in that company just has to be worth more and more.

What these people overlook is that the stock of ever a super-company is a good investment only when its current price is reasonable, if not low. Put another way, no stock can possibly be a good buy at any price.

The failure to recognize the difference between a stock and a company is all but universal among private investors. This is odd because the average American is usually quite price-conscious. Before buying a television set, for instance, he will often shop from store to store just to save $10 or $20. But when he's impressed with a popular company and is in the mood to invest, he buys its stock whether it is priced right or not.

True, few people regard the purchase of a TV set as an investment, and few expect the value of the set to grow. Stocks, on the other hand, are supposed to increase in value. But it's not hard to understand why a stock of a good company can be a bad investment. If an ever-increasing number of investors keep buying a popular stock, its price must eventually become much too high relative to the company's assets, earning power and dividend payments, as well as to other investment vehicles.

To be sure, an overpriced stock is not precluded from rising further. As long as the demand for that stock keeps exceeding the supply, its market quotation will climb. But sooner or later, everyone who is impressed with that company will have bought the stock. Once such a point is reached, demand for that issue vanishes. If only one shareholder finds it necessary to sell his holdings, supply will exceed demand, and the stock price will drop.

In reality, though, demand does not have to be fully exhausted before the upward trend of a popular stock is arrested or reversed. Especially with issues having widespread ownership, there are always many shareholders interested in selling. All it takes to reverse an uptrend is for supply to exceed demand.

Meanwhile, results of the last few years have made it abundantly clear that in the stock market, supply and demand are elastic. The higher a stock climbs, the greater the number of shares offered for sale. Unless the increased supply can be fully offset by increased demand, even stocks of great companies will retreat.

If buying a stock merely because 1) the company is "good" or 2) its earnings are expected to rise does not constitute sound investment, is buying a good company *plus* good earnings prospects any better? No. Even for the bluest of blue chips that boast unquestionably superior earnings growth records, demand cannot exceed supply forever.

Nevertheless, buying super companies with super earnings growth at any price was precisely what the freewheeling money managers at the big banks were doing in recent years. To them, it appeared, investing in the top companies of leading growing industries was all it took to insure investment success. Some went so far as to regard their Favorite Fifty as "one decision" stocks. All they had to do was decide when and how many shares to buy; they never had to concern themselves with when to sell.

The sharp drop suffered by the institutional darlings in 1974 has, of course, gone a long way toward debunking this one-decision theory But even before that, simple common sense had made it clear that the investment policy of those money managers was illogical as well as imprudent.

If an industry is to continue growing at a rapid pace, the market for that industry can be expected to broaden, so that more and more opportunities would become available to new firms in the field. Why, then, buy the shares of the industry leader? In an ever-expanding market, secondary companies can usually score greater percentage growth.

Normally, it's safer to invest only in the top companies of an industry because they typically enjoy strong financial positions and are therefore better able to survive major economic contractions. During the depression of the 1930's, any number of secondary companies with less than robust balance sheets became insolvent. But if the banks' money managers did anticipate a serious economic contraction, they should have avoided buying overpriced stocks of so-called growth companies altogether.

At any rate, the upshot is that buying stocks just because of favorable monetary developments, healthy earnings prospects and/or exciting corporate images does not constitute sound investment. Only when these and other factors combine to bring about a favorable supply-and-demand relationship do timely investment opportunities emerge.

CHAPTER 5

Are Charts Better Than Tea Leaves?

SINCE ECONOMIC AND MONETARY research, like personal feeling, does not directly contribute to good investment timing, should one turn to technical analysis?

Other than for those who engage in in-and-out trading, technical analysis is usually frowned upon by most investors. To them, analyzing price charts, odd-lot statistics, margin debt, etc. is no better than reading tea leaves. Ironically, of the various investment approaches, technical analysis actually comes closest to studying supply and demand.

Unfortunately, most stock market technicians—instead of understanding the logic behind their tools—interpret indicators mechanically. As a result, they don't really have very many more hits than misses. Moreover, like economists, they are almost always wrong at major turning points, the very time when investors need professional help most.

One barometer of how well technicians have done in the past is the record of investment advisory services—or market letters, as they are commonly known. The reason is that most such services base their opinions on technical analysis. That, in turn, is attributable partly to the fact that many publishers, instead of making lots of money in the market, are of limited means themselves and therefore do not have the capability of engaging in in-depth fundamental research.

There are literally hundreds of market letters available. Many are tip sheets, designed for the gullible. But there are several dozen which have enough substance to attract some following, and they are regularly monitored by a firm called Investor's Intelligence. Every week this Larchmont, New York-based company calculates the percentages of advisory services that are currently bullish, bearish or "correction" (somewhere in between).

Ideally, of course, an investment advisor should be most bearish when the market is at its peak and most bullish when the market is at its bottom. Only then can he help his clients properly prepare for the ensuing market decline or upswing.

But this is what the record shows. When the Dow Jones industrial average registered its all-time high in early 1973, over 60% of market letters were outright bullish, while only 15% were outright bearish; the rest were just wishy-washy. Conversely, in late May of 1970, when the Dow culminated an 18-month decline by dropping below 650, less than 30% of market letters were bullish, while nearly 60% were bearish.

The performance of these technically oriented market letters was a little better in December 1974, when the DJIA was at its second important bear market low of well below 600. But even then, less than 40% of such services were bullish while nearly 50% were still outright bearish.

In all fairness, many advisory services were probably on the right side of the market more often than not. They tend to be conspicuously wrong only at major turning points. This is because the nature of their work causes them to be trend followers. Chartists, for example, never acknowledge that a new market trend is in existence until long after that trend has been clearly established.

During the bull market heydays, this trend-following practice was no handicap. Broad price advances often ran for years, while significant turning points were few and far between. But in past decades, the market has fluctuated so widely and so frequently that votaries of the trend followers have found themselves severely whipsawed.

As I pointed out earlier, however, technical analysis actually comes closest to studying changes in the supply and demand relationship. Like economic and monetary research, therefore, this study can be put to good use if it is applied with some common sense.

Not all market indicators are meaningful, to be sure. A good number of them are absolutely nonsensical, having been created by market-letter writers strictly for sales-promotional purposes. But many approaches do have some logical background.

The Dow Theory for identifying market trends, for instance, is perhaps one of the most cherished theories among technicians. Supposedly, it helps analysts differentiate primary bull and bear markets from minor interim corrections. Since that theory was introduced some decades ago, many of its disciples have made some brilliant calls. Unfortunately, the Dow Theory has also caused interpreters to flash many a false signal.

As I see it, the Dow Theory is just a back-door method of finding out the overall supply-and-demand trend in the stock market. For instance, the theory contends that for a given market trend to be valid, a significant move made by the Dow Jones industrial average must be confirmed by a similar move by the railroad (now transportation) average. If the two averages diverge for any length of time, a major trend reversal may be in prospect. If a reversal of one average does occur and is echoed by the other, then a new trend is said to be in progress.

What the Dow Theory is saying, in effect, is that when stock prices advance across the board, total demand exceeds total supply, and the ongoing bull market is likely to continue. But when one segment of the market moves ahead while another segment declines, total demand may no longer be larger than total supply. Investors may just be selling one group of equities to buy another. Thus, the bull market is in danger of being reversed. Should all major groups begin to show a declining trend, total supply must have become greater than total demand, and a bear market has started.

The reason why the Dow Theory is based on the Dow Jones

industrial and railroad averages is evidently because when it was introduced in the old days, those were the only two indexes readily available to measure stock performance. (The utility group, representing "income stocks" only, is not supposed to reflect the typical equity.) Unfortunately, the 30 stocks that make up the industrial average and the 20 issues that make up the transportation average do not always epitomize the general market. This fact is especially conspicuous in recent years. As a result, market signals based strictly on those averages have frequently turned out wrong.

But if my interpretation of the logic behind the Dow Theory is right, then why put so much weight on those two Dow Jones averages? Nowadays, there are far more comprehensive statistics available to reflect more directly the price action of the cross-section of the market and the overall supply and demand situation.

Unlike reading tea leaves, there is logic in analyzing price charts, too. Let's suppose a certain stock has been selling between 30 and 35 for an extended period of time. The inference to be drawn then is that those investors who are interested in this stock have considered a price of 32 to 33 to be fair. Hence, whenever the stock dropped to 30, demand would pick up and the supply would shrink, causing the stock to bounce upward. And when the stock approached the 35 level, the opposite would occur and the issue would retreat thereafter.

Now, if that stock suddenly jumps to, say, 37 on exceptionally heavy trading volume, something new has evidently developed to cause enough investors to realize that the stock's fair value has increased. That new development may or may not be known to the public. But if it is valid, a new supply-and-demand relationship has been created. This is why many chart readers would consider such a breakout a buy signal.

The danger of acting on buy or sell signals flashed by price and volume movements alone is that many such breakouts turn out to be false. If so, a trader rushing to buy the stock in the example above at 37 would only see his holdings dropping back to the low 30's shortly thereafter.

This danger is quite real in recent years, because many money managers supervising institutional portfolios control enormous buying power. Some of these professionals are notoriously impatient. As a result, a single buy or sell order from any one of these money managers can send a stock's quotation rising above or falling below its normal range temporarily. For that reason, it's far safer to first determine from other research approaches whether a stock is about to go up or down and then monitor the price chart for timing purposes.

Statistics on odd-lot transactions are another example of how technical analysis can be helpful if the user is flexible enough to adjust to changing conditions. In the old days, these data were regarded by followers as a contrary-opinion guide. Whenever net purchases by investors trading in less-than-100-share lots increased markedly, according to those experts, a major market decline would soon follow. The opposite held true whenever odd-lotters sold heavily on balance.

For years, this theory worked quite well. The logic is that heavy buying by small investors reflects rampant speculation, and intense speculation is always corrected subsequently by a substantial market decline. Conversely, heavy selling by this group mirrors widespread panic; and a panic-stricken market is almost always followed by a healthy recovery.

In recent years, however, traders using odd-lot data in that conventional way would have been seriously misled. Unlike Wall Street experts, small investors have actually succeeded in selling at the top and buying at the bottom. Specifically, in the final weeks of 1972, just before the Dow Jones industrials made its all-time peak, the 10-day average of the odd-lot sales-to-purchases ratio reached the highest level ever. By way of contrast, in the middle of 1970 and then again in the fall of 1974, when the Dow was down to around the 600 range, that sales-to-purchase ratio had dropped precipitously.

This dramatic improvement in the overall performance of small investors has not, in any way, negated the usefulness of odd-lot statistics. I myself have found this indicator highly helpful.

Why has the conventional interpretation of odd-lot data become obsolete? Statistics from other sources revealed long ago that an underlying change in the public investing pattern was taking place. Back in the 1940's and 1950's, private *investors*—both odd-lotters and round-lotters—were consistently net stock buyers. As I pointed out earlier, most private individuals do not monitor the economy. They invest systematically. Hence, until recent years when their confidence was shaken, their sales-to-purchase ratio held rather steady.

Consequently, the sudden changes in the odd-lot sales-to-purchase ratio in the old days were largely attributable to the odd-lot *speculators*. Significantly, uninformed speculators do buy and sell at precisely the wrong time. Their judgment is always dominated by fear or greed.

Since the late 1960's, however, many small speculators have been scared out of the market by bad losses. Most others have promoted themselves into trading in round-lots, no doubt a sign of the affluent society. As a result, those who still engage in odd-lot transactions are predominantly serious, long-term investors.

Since serious private investors transacting in both round lots and odd lots are probably motivated to buy or sell stocks by the same factors, the odd-lot sales-to-purchase ratio has thus become an index of what all serious private individuals are doing.

As a group, private investors play a very strong role in influencing the total demand for and supply of stocks, having more money and stock holdings than financial institutions and speculators combined. (The latter groups turn over their holdings more often, however.) It stands to reason, therefore, that heavy odd-lot sales nowadays foreshadow a market decline and heavy odd-lot purchases precede a market rise.

Thus, as you can see, technical analysis is indeed useful; it is not at all a pseudo-science. That's why I keep scores of indicators under surveillance and The Holt Investment Advisory discusses the market's technical position in every issue. But only those technical indicators that are supported by logic should be used—in conjunction with other research and common sense.

CHAPTER 6

Let's Deflate a Few Myths

UP TO THIS POINT, I have explained why economic, monetary and technical analysis, though all essential, are inadequate for successful investing when they are applied to study the market in the conventional way. They must be employed logically and flexibly. Thus, under the Total Investment Approach, we integrate these various analyses and then decide how they interact to affect the total demand for and the total supply of stocks.

Before getting into that approach, though, there are still a few popular myths which we must first dispose of. Otherwise, they too are likely to keep distorting your judgment in the future.

Because the 1973-74 market tumble occurred at a time when the U.S. was suffering from double-digit inflation, investors have lately come to believe that inflation is bad for stocks. Ironically, up until just a few years ago, common stock had been universally considered to be an ideal hedge against inflation. Is inflation really bullish or bearish for equities? Directly, neither. Indirectly, it is sometimes bullish and sometimes bearish.

Admittedly, that answer sounds like typical Wall Street double-talk. But let me show you the logic behind it.

Strictly speaking, of course, inflation reflects (or results from) a decline in the purchasing power of the money in use. When it happens, the price of just about everything expressed in that currency rises. Corporate assets are no exceptions. Since common shares represent equities in a company's assets, inflation thus directly increases the underlying asset value of all stocks.

Nevertheless, this underlying asset value, like the book value, seldom plays a significant role in determining the market quotation of a stock. The fact is, in inflationary times, going corporations are hardly ever liquidated; their assets are hardly ever distributed to shareholders. (By way of contrast, many companies are involuntarily liquidated during periods of depression and deflation.) The fact that inflation has increased the market value of corporate assets is thus academic to the shareholder. That's why *directly,* inflation is neither bullish or bearish.

Elementary though it may sound, this is something many investors often overlook or forget. When a person hedges against inflation by buying rare goods or real property, he can reasonably expect to eventually liquidate those holdings at inflated prices. But he cannot do so by buying a stock unless he has good reason to believe that the company involved will indeed be liquidated, and that the liquidation proceeds will indeed come close to the inflated asset value.

Indirectly, though, inflation can be bullish for stocks—sometimes. A price rise reflects an excess of demand over supply for the service or goods involved. In such an environment, a seller's market exists. As sellers of goods and/or services, most corporations are therefore better able to increase profits and dividends in an inflationary period. That, in turn, attracts demand for their stocks.

On the other hand, the general increase in the demand for goods and services that brings about inflation in the first place is usually financed by mushrooming debt. A sustained rise in borrowing invariably results in higher interest rates. And higher interest rates not only inflate the cost of doing business but also entice investors to switch into securities that provide higher returns than stocks.

Furthermore, inflation also swells the cost of replacing inventories and capital plants, thereby depressing corporate real cash profits. Accordingly, inflation, especially if it runs at a rate faster than that budgeted by corporate managements, can sometimes be bearish for stocks.

Again, the point to remember is that to appraise the impact of inflation—or, for that matter, anything else—investors should not follow any rigid rule but should again use common sense and understand the prevailing circumstances. Always try to find out first whether this or that development or prospect has already found reflection in the market's supply and demand relationship.

Another popular myth that has proved to be particularly damaging to the lay investor in recent years is the belief that the government can control or manage the nation's monetary and economic conditions. Academic economists can probably present thesis upon thesis to prove or disprove this point. But here again, why get involved with lengthy debates over fancy economic theories? Just a little simple logic will go a long way toward clarifying the picture.

For instance, the most widely accepted belief among consumers, investors and businessmen alike is that the Federal Reserve Board sets the level of interest rates. Time and again in recent years, monetary experts in Congress have blamed the FRB for having pegged interest rates too high. I concede that the Fed can probably nudge interest rates in one direction or another slightly and for a short while. But it certainly cannot change the underlying forces that determine true free-market rates.

It's probably an understatement to say that all politicians, as well as all businessmen and consumers, want to see the interest rate as low as possible. Only financial institutions and those "unconscionable rich" with cash to invest want high interest income; but they don't control many votes. It is also true that, despite its "independent status," the Federal Reserve Board has always strived to accommodate politicians, businessmen and consumers.

If the FRB indeed has the power to control interest rates, logic would dictate that those rates would be maintained at bargain levels. After all, the cheap money available in the mid-Forties did pave the way for spectacular postwar economic expansion throughout the world. But as I pointed out earlier in this book, both long-term and short-term rates have trended upward persistently for three decades and are now many, many times higher than those prevailing at the end of World War II.

It may be argued that the Fed has purposely allowed interest rates to rise in order to avoid the outbreak of inflation. If so, the Board has certainly done a miserable job. We all know that in 1973-74 prices rose at double-digit rates.

What has happened to gold is another example showing that free-market forces are stronger than the governments of all leading countries combined. Until the late 1960's, the U.S. Treasury and virtually all major foreign central banks had insisted that the dollar was as good as gold and the then $35-an-ounce official price of the metal was untouchable. They meant every word of those official assurances. But most of you probably know what has happened since: although it has declined from the December 1974 peak, the free-market price is still many times the $35 rate.

As far back as the mid-1960's, when inflation was accelerating to the 4% annual rate, politicians have been talking about fighting inflation. The war against inflation was escalated by one Administration after another, by Republican and Democratic presidents alike. But the more the government fought inflation, the faster prices rose. The inflation spiral was finally dampened only when a major economic slowdown finally emerged in late 1974—a slowdown *not* wanted by the government.

The recognition that the government, no matter how powerful it is, cannot control free-market forces is important because only then can investors truly appraise how government action will distort economic and monetary conditions and how those conditions will influence the investment markets.

By the same token, investors should also remember that neither the Wall Street establishment nor major financial institutions can control stock prices. Because they turn over their portfolios actively, institutional investors have in recent years accounted for a lion's share of daily stock transactions. As a result, the public has gotten the impression that "big money" actually controls stock prices. Not at all.

The fact, again, is that private individuals still own by far the bulk of the nation's financial assets. The manner in which they allocate their liquid holdings among various investment vehicles plays the key role in influencing security prices.

In this connection, I thought you may find the following anecdote amusing. A few years back, the Holt Investment Advisory recommended the short sale of Avon Products at around 100. Shortly, thereafter, a financial writer commented in a leading newspaper that "only a fool" would do such a thing. Avon, that expert argued, was such an institutional darling that the professionals would never allow the stock to fall.

In 1972 and 1973, financial institutions apparently did try to artificially support that issue. But free market forces were more powerful. By mid-1974, when the Advisory advised the closing out of that position, the short sale had generated a profit of nearly 50%.

Finally, there is this ultimate myth, obviously promoted by Wall Street: your stock broker is your best source of investment advice. In our free enterprise system, those who produce the best products and give the best services are usually those who have the greatest incentive to do so. Note that stock brokers derive almost all their income from commissions. Their incentive, therefore, is to induce you to transact in your account as often as possible. Many brokers can be highly successful in persuading you to do just that. But in no way is this consistent with sound investment practices.

Actually, not many brokers have a deep knowledge in economics, in monetary developments or even in the securities they recommend. You can't blame them; giving advice is not their job. Besides, most of them are supposedly backed by the research departments of their firms. But brokerage firms themselves also depend heavily on commission income. It's perfectly reasonable to assume, therefore, that the analyses circulated by their research departments are also aimed primarily at stimulating transactions. Building capital for clients is just a secondary consideration. Those analysts who don't turn out many reports with "buy" recommendations don't keep their jobs for long these days.

Instead of looking to your broker for advice, therefore, depend on him only to execute your orders efficiently. Be especially wary of such commission-generating recommendations as: "Buy some more now to average down your cost," "Sell now since you already have a 3-point profit," "Place a stop-loss order just below the present price," or "Sell against the box to protect your gains."

In short, don't be a tool of your broker. Let him really work for his commission income.

CHAPTER 7

What's So Sacred About P/E Ratios?

THE VALUE OF price/earnings ratios is another myth that has misled investors for generations. Unfortunately, no matter how badly investors are hurt by this guide, the myth persists. Indeed, earnings multiples have actually gained in stature in recent years. The press is now printing these ratios along with daily stock quotations.

What is the price/earnings ratio, anyway? It is the numerical relationship between a stock's current price and its annual earnings—and nothing more. As an investment guide, it is no more useful than any other number from zero to infinity.

Why then have brokers and stock analysts relied so heavily on that ratio? Because it is the handiest tool they can use to rationalize their recommendations.

As I noted earlier, few brokers have much research ability; so they have to talk the way stock analysts talk. But most of the so-called securities or financial analysts are not really analysts of *finance*, or of *securities* either. The less experienced, in my opinion, can best be described as glorified statisticians, the more proficient as good *company* or *industry* analysts.

For instance, the typical in-depth institutional research report contains tens of thousands of words and figures and runs page after page. (Brokerage firms have learned that a 100-page analysis saying nothing is worth more "soft dollars" from institutional clients than one page of concise study.) Chances are that 99% of such a report is devoted to discussing the company or the industry involved. But when it comes to judging whether the stock is attractive or not, the study may just insert a short phrase about the earnings multiple.

Thus, it's common to find two analysts, analyzing the same company and talking to the same corporate public relations officer, producing substantially the same sort of "in depth" analysis. But if they have opposite preconceived opinions about the stock, their conclusions might read something like this: 1) "Since this stock is now selling at only 15 times earnings, down from its 10-year average of 22, we recommend purchase for long-term growth" vs. 2) "With the stock selling at 15 times earnings, sharply higher than the DJIA's multiple, we recommend immediate sale."

The irony here, of course, is that most Wall Street analysts themselves don't know the difference between companies and stocks. Many analysts do indeed do a thorough job in studying individual corporations and industries. Some even project earnings down to the pennies three to five years ahead. But when evaluating the stocks of those companies, the best they can do is to compare P/E's.

Again, you can't really blame them. To properly evaluate any security issue, the analyst must take into consideration not only what other stocks are selling for, but also factors that might affect the entire investment market. He has to anticipate developments in the bond markets, the short-term money and credit markets, the foreign exchange market, etc. In other words, the "financial analyst" must have expert knowledge of what's happening in the world of finance. To do that, he must be able to make, or have access to, realistic economic and monetary forecasts. But the chances are that he knows little about economic analysis, nor can he get realistic forecasts from conventional economists, especially those hired by brokerage firms.

Wall Street analysts are quite clever in using P/E ratios to rationalize their positions, to be sure. They come up with some fancy statistical comparisons. Supposedly, a stock selling at a multiple lower than that of another in the same industry or of similar quality, or lower than its own past norm, is attractively priced, and vice versa. But that is dangerously misleading.

In an analysis titled "Beware of Those Bargains," The Holt Investment Advisory advised investors back in the spring of 1973 to resist the urge to buy low P/E stocks. At that time, only a little over 60 issues listed on the New York Stock Exchange were selling at multiples of less than 6.5. Mainly because those "bargains" were paying small or no dividends and because we were convinced that the investing public was becoming more and more income-conscious, we pointed out that they were really overpriced.

In the one and a half years that ensued, the Dow Jones industrials plunged over 300 points, or roughly 35%. But most of those 60-odd "cheap" issues plunged 50% to 75%.

Some skeptics may argue that the 1973-74 market collapse was unusually bad; it's not fair to use that period as an example. But the worthlessness of price/earnings ratios as an investment guide dates back far before the recent market collapse. Take, for instance, early 1966, when the Dow Jones industrials first approached the 1000 level. At that time, the average was selling at only 16.8 times the earnings of the 30 component companies. By way of comparison, the average P/E for the DJIA over the three preceding years had been 18.2; and in late 1961, it had attained a peak multiple of close to 24.

By Wall Street's standards, the Dow average would have been judged as "attractively priced and should be bought for superior growth" in early 1966; certainly, it should have been "retained in conservative accounts for the long pull." Yet if an investor could indeed have bought a share of the Dow Jones industrial average then, he would have lost some 25% by October that year. Even today—nearly ten years later—he would still have a good-sized paper loss.

In retrospect, many analysts now acknowledge that earnings multiples were indeed too high back in the 1960's. The implication is that there is a certain level or range that is normal, fair or appropriate. But there can be no such standard. True, with the help of computers, statisticians can survey the price/earnings ratios prevailing over past decades and come up with an average. But for investment guidance purposes, such a figure is of no significance.

Depending on the general economic, monetary and market conditions—or, more specifically, on the potential demand of and supply for stocks—any given earnings multiple can be too high at one time and too low at another. There is no reason whatsoever to believe that a stock with an above-average P/E won't go up or that a stock with a below-average multiple won't go down.

Let's look at what happened to American Telephone & Telegraph, the most widely held common stock in the world. This issue is particularly suitable for our illustration here because its long-term earnings growth has by and large been quite consistent. Thus, few analysts or shareholders have had much difficulty making reasonably accurate earnings projections. In other words, changes in the multiple at which the company's earnings were capitalized by the market in the past could not have been caused by "uncertainties" over the company's earnings prospect.

In the 1940's and 1950's, the P/E ratio of this stock stayed quite close to 15. Then, reflecting a sharp rise in the stock's price, the multiple jumped to around 18 by the end of 1960. According to conventional wisdom, AT&T, selling close to 50 then, was distinctly overpriced.

What happened thereafter? In the ensuing year, the stock climbed 20 points more; and in four years, it had scored an overall gain of over 50%.

Coincidentally, AT&T was again selling at about 18 times earnings five years later, at the end of 1965. This time, the current multiple was well below the average of over 20 times for the few years immediately theretofore. Was the stock a good buy then? Not at all. By the following summer, it had fallen more than 10 points to approximately 50; and by the middle of 1970, it was selling close to 40.

This AT&T case history, which is by no means unique, points up the danger of substituting P/E ratios for investment judgment.

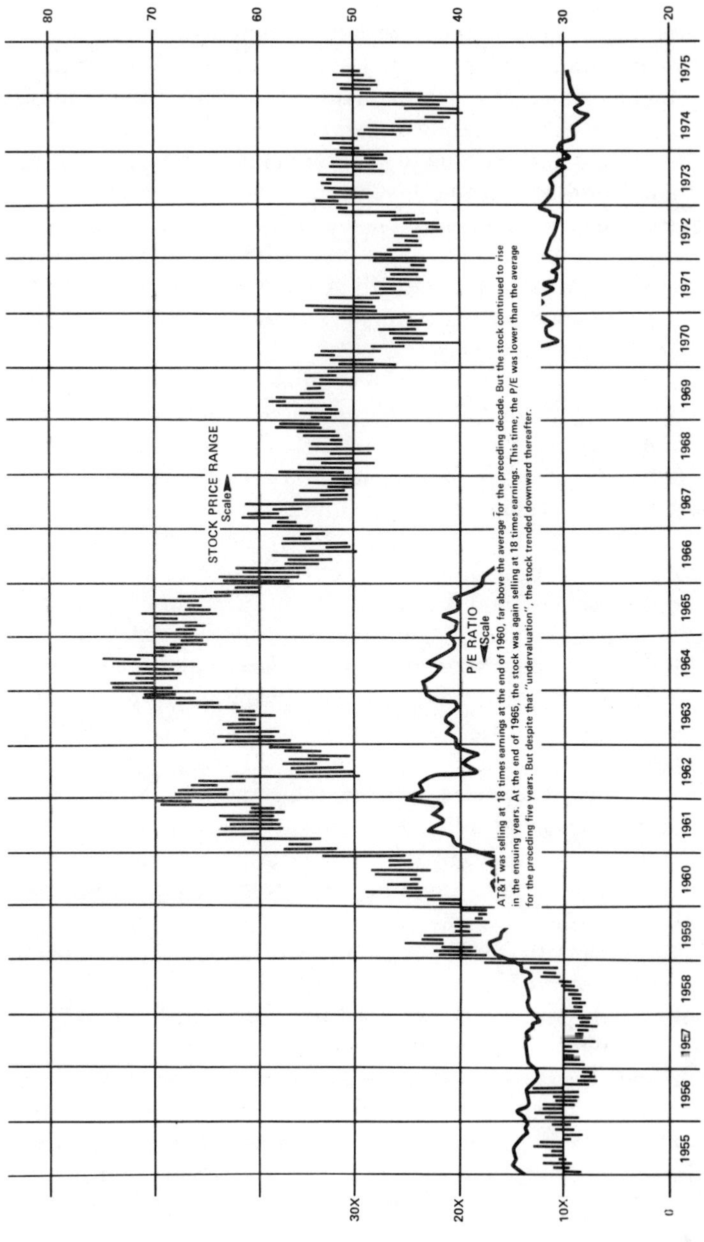
STOCK PRICE RANGE
Scale
P/E RATIO
Scale
AT&T was selling at 18 times earnings at the end of 1960, far above the average for the preceding decade. But the stock continued to rise in the ensuing years. At the end of 1965, the stock was again selling at 18 times earnings. This time, the P/E was lower than the average for the preceding five years. But despite that "undervaluation", the stock trended downward thereafter.
1955
1956
1957
1958
1959
1960
1961
1962
1963
1964
1965
1966
1967
1968
1969
1970
1971
1972
1973
1974
1975
80
70
60
50
40
30
20
30X
20X
10X
0

In the main, stock prices are heavily influenced by investors' sentiment. Rather than moving toward some recent norm, this sentiment—which governs the amount of funds flowing into the stock market in general and individual stocks in particular—tends to swing from one extreme to another in long-term cycles.

Aside from the fact that investor psychology is hard to predict ahead of time, P/E ratios are meaningless also because the quality of earnings at individual companies often varies markedly. There have been efforts to standardize accounting procedures, but the bases on which reported profits are computed still differ greatly from one company to another.

The variance sometimes reflects differences in the nature of the business of individual companies or industries. But there also are major disparities in accounting practices relating to, for example, the treatment of depreciation, inventory, investment tax credits, research and development expenditures, and related items.

It is not uncommon, therefore, for a company following conservative accounting practice to write off all research and development expenses and so-called make-ready costs and to use accelerated depreciation and amortization schedules to report much lower earnings than an identical firm that uses more liberal methods. Yet the first company, enjoying a larger cash flow because of smaller tax liabilities, would actually be in a better financial position to pay dividends and to work toward future growth.

The quality of reported earnings is also affected by the balance sheet. Though most Wall Street analysts scarcely discuss the financial position of companies they study, the capital structure of a corporation has a great bearing on the amount of earnings available for dividend payments or future expansion. For example, a company that is debt-heavy must allocate a substantial portion of future profits for repaying creditors, leaving less money available for pay-outs to common shareholders. For that reason, such earnings should not be capitalized as generously—at least by informed investors—as those of a debt-free concern.

The cyclical nature of a company's business also affects the quality of current earnings. The boom-time net of, say, a consumer durable goods manufacturer is, in all probability, considerably higher than its normal earning power. As a result, such earnings are not taken seriously by savvy investors.

THE HOLT INVESTMENT ADVISORY

MONTHLY FEATURE

Rating 200 Widely-Held Stocks

WITH THE AID of electronic computers, the Advisory regularly rates 200 widely-held stocks for those investors who prefer to make their own selections of stocks to buy, sell or short.

The **Relative Value Rating** reveals whether a stock is overpriced, fairly priced or underpriced on the basis of the company's financial strength as well as operating results. An "A" rating means that the stock is deeply undervalued; a "C" rating, fairly valued; and an "E" rating, grossly overvalued. Note the word "Relative". In other words, these ratings compare the stocks with the market in general.

Current Yield, of course, is the indicated annual dividend as a percent of the recent stock price. Frequently, it also represents the cost of carrying a short position in that stock. The **Relative Yield Index** relates the stock's current yield to interest rates prevailing in the money market. Generally speaking, the higher this Index reads, the greater is the stock's defensive quality in a down market.

Very often, fundamentally underpriced stocks keep declining and overpriced issues keep rising. This is partly because many financial institutions engage in heavy buying or selling without paying much attention to values. As a result, market action nowadays is heavily influenced by technical factors (near-term supply and demand). Before taking any action, therefore, investors are well advised to ascertain whether the equity position of their portfolio is in line with the Recommended Investment Strategy discussed on the front page of each issue of the Advisory. Also, check the Advisory's analysis of the market's technical stance.

STOCK	RECENT PRICE	RELATIVE VALUE	CURRENT YIELD	RELATIVE YIELD INDEX	STOCK	RECENT PRICE	RELATIVE VALUE	CURRENT YIELD	RELATIVE YIELD INDEX
Airco Inc.	20	B	4.5%	64	Commun. Satellite	45	D	2.2%	32
Alcan Aluminium	25	D	3.2%	45	Consolidated Edison	14	A	8.6%	122
Allied Chemical	39	D	4.6%	65	Consumers Power	18	A	11.1%	158
Allis Chalmers	12	A	2.2%	31	Continental Can	25	C	7.2%	102
Alum. Co. of America	47	E	2.9%	40	Continental Oil	67	D	3.0%	42
Amax, Inc.	56	[illegible]	[illegible]	[illegible]	[illegible]	[illegible]	[illegible]	[illegible]	0
									66

This is a sample of how The Holt Investment Advisory regularly rates 200 widely-held stocks. Note that no price/earnings ratios are listed. Instead, Relative Value, Current Yield and Relative Yield Index are featured.

For a given company, the quality of earnings can also vary from one period to the next. There are many types of indirect operating expenses that are usually charged directly to current income, but the benefits derived from them are spread over a period of time. The most conspicuous item in this category, perhaps, is the cost of drilling or mining for natural resources. Frequently, a sharp increase in such outlays can sharply depress current results, while substantially enhancing underlying values. Other expenditures in this category include advertising, product development, plant start-ups, and employee-training programs.

The upshot is that the quality of earnings is influenced by a wide variety of factors. Some are measurable, others are almost totally intangible. Given this state of affairs, P/E ratios are of little use as a determinant of stock value.

CHAPTER 8

Why Do the Rich Get Richer?

IN THE LAST FEW chapters, I've discussed why you should erase from your memory bank the myths and unworkable rules that characterize Wall Street's conventional wisdom. I cannot overemphasize how important it is for you to do so. Otherwise, the myths will distort your judgment, perhaps subconsciously, time and again.

Once liberated from those myths, you can proceed to build capital with the Total Investment Approach.

But to build capital, of course you need capital. If there's any truth to the saying that "the rich get richer"—and I believe there is—it's mainly because the rich have more money to make money with. And, whether in business or in investment, they are willing to take calculated risks. So, to embark on a successful capital-building program, you too must have adequate capital to start with, capital that's *working actively* for you. And you must be willing and able to assume more than minimal risks.

Agreeing to accept increased risks is easy. But you have to be honest with yourself. Many investors claim that they know what they're doing when they buy highly speculative issues. But once losses hit them, they become extremely upset. Remember, when you take risks, you will inevitably have occasional losses. You must learn to accept such losses gracefully. Perhaps it will help to remember that, over a period of time, assuming somewhat higher risks—*intelligent* risks—often results in greater capital growth.

Don't confuse capital building with outright gambling, however. Betting in Las Vegas or at the racetrack also involves enormous risks. But taking those risks does not give the players superior capital growth potential; the odds there are stacked against them. In the securities markets, the odds are very much in favor of the alert investor.

Unfortunately, because of their bad experience in recent years, many people have since sworn off investing in stocks and have put their capital in real estate or in savings accounts. Earlier in this book, I pointed out why buying real estate for investment purposes is not advisable so late in the inflation cycle. Idling too much capital in a savings account is not much better.

It is, of course, prudent to have some ready cash around for a rainy day. However, immobilizing more money than you need to meet emergencies constitutes an inefficient use of capital. (Besides, there is some question as to whether all savings institutions are really as financially sound as they are supposed to be.)

The fact is, no enterprising businessman would settle for a return on invested capital of just 5% or 6% from his business. Similarly, no good financial institution would set that kind of return as its long-term goal. After all, an increase of just a few percentage points in the annual rate of return makes an enormous difference over a period of years.

To illustrate, a 5% annual return compounded for 10 years comes to only 63%. But a 10% annual return compounded for 10 years equals 159%; a 15% annual return, 304%; and a 20% annual return, 519%.

For that reason, those who can afford to take some risks should always put their money to work harder than just collecting savings-bank interest. This doesn't mean speculating blindly. In the long run, a carefully supervised investment program should yield more than income from a savings bank. If it's really difficult to earn more than a 5% return, savings institutions wouldn't be so eager to give you a free radio or toaster just to get hold of your money.

Keeping your capital frozen in investments acquired long years ago is even worse. Chances are, over the years, while the capital was locked in, it did not even earn a savings-bank return.

Many investors have been holding on to losers simply because they hate to take losses. Retaining "good" stocks for the long pull and riding through interim market valleys may work perfectly well in a sustained bull market. After every market drop in the 1940's and 1950's, for example, almost all but the very worst stocks sooner or later advanced to new highs. But in the absence of an across-the-board and sustained market advance, inaction is not just impractical; it is demoralizing as well.

Look through a long-term chart book. You'll notice that hundreds of securities have been trending downward in the last eight or ten years. Many shareholders have undoubtedly held those issues all the way down, eternally hoping throughout those years that "the worst is over and a recovery cannot be far behind."

Had those shareholders liquidated their holdings years ago and put the capital to work more intelligently, they might well have experienced real recovery instead of continued capital attrition. To add insult to injury, every time they thought about their unfortunate investments during those years, they probably got a bad case of depression.

There are times, of course, when certain stocks are temporarily undervalued and retention for eventual recovery is justified. But more often than not, the original reasons for buying those issues were either faulty or have been invalidated by subsequent developments.

Thus, refusing to face up to the fact that the losses, whether taken or not, *already* exist, may actually endanger whatever capital is left. By contrast, once the loss is taken, the investor should be able to use that capital more gainfully elsewhere. As a bonus, he will also experience some psychological relief, and may even realize tax benefits.

Speaking of taxes, many other long-term investors have found themselves "locked in" by capital gains. Although stock prices have come down considerably since the late 1960's, most issues are still standing far above the levels prevailing from the 1930's through the 1950's. Many of those investors who hold stocks originally bought then have thus been reluctant to sell, lest they incur large capital-gains tax liabilities.

Substantial though such taxes may be, it is often far cheaper to pay the taxes on *just the capital gains* than to risk a much larger loss *on the total capital involved.* This applies even now to those glamour issues artificially bid up by the big banks.

Actually, as soon as a stock advances from its purchase price, a potential tax liability accrues. The liability can be eliminated either by nailing down the profit and paying the taxes—or by waiting for the stock to retreat to its original purchase price, which of course erases the paper profit. Obviously, the first alternative is better. So, it is again a matter of facing up to reality.

Another way of looking at the frozen-in-by-taxes situation is to consider the tax liability as a kind of interest-free loan from the government. During the bull-market heyday, it was a good idea to ride the market with Uncle Sam's money. But stocks no longer go up automatically. Carrying an equity position just because of an interest-free loan can be penny-wise-pound-foolish.

Tying up your capital in companies you happen to like is also a no-no. All too often, investors retain certain stocks because they have "fallen in love" with them. But personal feelings should never be allowed to influence investment decisions. The corporation issuing the shares is itself a non-human entity incapable of emoting. And the managements of most firms hardly care who their shareholders are—unless a proxy fight is threatening. So, why engage in a one-sided love affair?

Whether your capital should remain invested in a present holding should really be based only on whether that investment continues to offer satisfactory growth potential *now.* How well or how poorly the stock has done in the past is, except for some technical considerations, of little significance.

In this connection, I might point out that it is also foolhardy to avoid certain stocks simply because of personal hangups. Some investors, for example, insist that they would never buy tobacco or defense stocks. Their reason: smoking and war are undesirable. This sort of moralizing doesn't make much sense. The investor who buys a tobacco stock does not in any way increase the number of people smoking; and the investor who avoids a defense stock does not prevent wars from breaking out.

In the open market, an investor buys shares from an existing holder, who is just a member of the investing public. The companies are not involved. Even if the investment boycott could succeed in depressing the stocks involved down to zero, the company itself remains perfectly healthy. The only victims are some innocent shareholders, including millions of non-smoking and peace-loving participants in pension and mutual funds.

Thus, if stocks of these or any other industries are expected to rise, capitalize on the move and invest in them. If you don't make money in them, someone else will. And if you are really against smoking and killing, wouldn't it be better to use part of your profits realized from those investments to help finance campaigns that reflect your views? In a war, there is nothing more gratifying than to destroy the enemy with weapons captured from him.

Summing up, to build capital you must have capital actively working for you and you must be financially and emotionally prepared to assume some risks. Investment success comes only after you understand and respect risk. Don't let your capital get locked in by unsatisfactory holdings. Gains or losses, taxes or emotion must never overcome your investment judgment. Always be the master of your capital.

Before I close this chapter, here are a few extra words for young people.

If you want to build up a nest egg, you must determine to regularly put aside some of your present income for capital-building purposes. This is not an easy decision to make, to be sure. Expenditures always seem to rise faster than income. It's hard enough not to go into debt, let alone to have money left over for savings. The fact, though, is that many people with modest incomes are indeed able to save regularly.

Now, if you put aside $2,000 a year out of your income for investing and then incur a $2,000 installment loan to buy a car, you are *not* saving. Instead, you are borrowing to play the market, and that's dangerous. Except in those rare cases when the reward-to-risk ratio is very much in your favor, your investment capital should be free and and clear of debt.

I am not saying that all of you must save and that nobody should incur installment loans. The use of credit is a fundamental part of our economic system. Without it, a large segment of the population would not be able to reap the harvest of their labor until they were too old to enjoy it. Nevertheless, if you do want to build capital, you'll just have to create a capital base—even if it means lowering your standard of living *now* in exchange for a much higher standard of living *later.*

CHAPTER 9

Kung Fu for Investing

KUNG FU, AS YOU may know, is the martial art of self-defense originated in old China. Unlike the conventional fighter, the master of Kung Fu never meets his adversary headlong. By being alert and flexible, he instead conserves his own energy and cleverly converts opposing forces to his advantage. Temporary reverses never upset him. Cool-headed at all all times, he varies his strategy to cope with changing conditions.

The principal behind Kung Fu is what the Total Investment Approach applies to protect and build capital. In an ever-rising bull market, one has to be pretty clumsy and unlucky not to have a winning strategy. But when the market is erratic or, worse yet, when it points downward, bull market tactics are simply inappropriate. Investors must learn to cope with and indeed capitalize on what may otherwise be adverse forces.

Take, for instance, the pension and retirement funds managed by conventional "experts." Relative to total assets, the equity holdings of these portfolios have trended upward persistently. Increasing the equity position *was* a sound policy when the long-run bull market was in progress. But since the late 1960's, the risks involved in equity investing have obviously mounted. Continuing to accumulate common stocks heavily during most of this period can hardly be regarded as prudent management.

The managers of these portfolios have, to be sure, made occasional changes in their investment policy to reflect their views of the economy or the market. Typically, they zero in on the cyclicals and the glamours when they expect business activities to rise. When they foresee a down market, they accumulate "defensive" stocks like foods and utilities.

On the surface, that policy of keeping in tune with the economy and the market seems smart enough. But if we stop and think about it, we see that it is in fact unwise.

For one thing, it assumes that just because the economy is pointing upward, the market price of cyclical and glamour stocks will go up. The fortunes of cyclical companies do usually improve with a business upturn, but their stocks may not. By the same token, the utility and food industries may be less adversely affected by a business contraction than automobiles and major appliance makers. But it does not necessary follow that in a bad market such "defensive" issues are sure to decline less than the popular averages. They could well have entered the bear market far more overpriced than the rest of the list.

Moreover, one doesn't *build* capital by *losing* less than the averages. Failing to foresee an approaching bear market is bad enough. But to anticipate a declining market by investing in stocks that will drop "only modestly" defies logic. Common sense dictates that the proper thing to do is to liquidate most, if not all, equity holdings and to reacquire them at much lower prices near the bear market bottom.

Granted, the big banks that manage the pension and retirement and other trust funds control so much stock that it is impossible for them to liquidate even a portion of their clients' positions without seriously upsetting the market. But at the very least, they could hold off new purchases of even defensive issues until the bear market is substantially over.

Of course, no one can predict for sure precisely when a bull or a bear market is beginning or ending. But this does not negate the need for a sensible investment policy—a policy that takes into consideration both the gain and the risk potentials.

Moreover, I have found that it is indeed possible to gain an insight into what the market will *probably* do by using Flow-of-Funds analysis, which will be discussed in the coming chapters. Obviously, the higher the probability for a rising market, the greater is the reward-to-risk ratio, and vice versa.

On the basis of probability, then, investors should adjust their equity positions from time to time. Thus, when a strongly advancing market is indicated, some 80% to 100% of investment funds may be allocated to equities and equity-related securities. As rising stock prices reduce the reward-to-risk ratio, the equity position should be scaled down. And when a declining market appears likely, the equity position should be substantially eliminated.

As stock prices tumble, the reward-to-risk ratio will improve. The thing to do then is to gradually reestablish your equity position so that when stock prices are at, or near, their bottom, your portfolio is substantially committed to equities.

"This theory may sound good on paper," the skeptic may say, "but can it be put into actual practice without the help of hindsight?" Yes. The published record of The Holt Investment Advisory proves this.

For the sake of simplicity, let's just examine the period between the spring of 1967 and the spring of 1970, although the record of the Advisory in many subsequent periods was actually better. That three-year period covered the last one and a half years of the longest primary bull market on record and the first one and a half years of the primary bear market that ensued. In short, that period witnessed the most critical stock market reversal in modern history.

To refresh your memory, let me point out that the Dow Jones industrial average was in the mid-800's at the start of that period. It subsequently rose to about 1000 by the end of 1968. Thereafter, it dropped until it reached the low 600's in the latter part of May 1970.

Now, let's look at the published record of The Holt Investment Advisory:

In May 1967, the Advisory told sophisticated investors to put "as much as 75% to 80%" of their investment capital in equities.

In October 1967, after the Dow-Jones industrials had risen above 920, the Advisory advised enterprising investors to reduce their equity holdings to "no more than 50%."

In early December 1968, Wall Street was bubbling with enthusiasm because the Dow was approaching 1000. But the Advisory recommended an equity position of only 40%. It further specified that "at least 25% . . . be invested in gold stocks, and only 15% . . . in other recommended stocks."

By the middle of May 1969, the Dow-Jones industrials, after some gyrations in the interim, had undergone a modest net decline—to around 970. Wall Street was still looking for 1000+; but the Advisory stated flatly, "No more than 25% of investment funds should remain in common stocks, the golds included."

By early February 1970, the Dow had already dropped more than 200 points. With that average standing just above 750, the Advisory told investors to "increase their equity position from 20% to 40%."

Three months after, in early May of 1970, the Dow-Jones industrials were another 50 points lower. The Advisory then told investors to "increase the equity position . . . to 60%."

As noted earlier, the market finally registered its 1970 low just a few weeks later. The June 5th issue of the Advisory published this recommendation: "We now recommend that those cash reserves previously set aside be put to work, increasing the equity position to 80%. (The other 20% of funds should remain in long-term bonds.)"

The above record thus shows that in those three crucial years when the market reached its postwar high and then suffered its first primary-bear-market break, the Advisory's recommended equity position changed from 75-80% to only 25% (including gold stocks) and then back up to 80%. It proves clearly that a logical investment policy—lowering the equity position when the risk is high and increasing it when the risk is low—can be implemented without the help of hindsight.

Note that in some of the recommendations quoted, there were some references to gold stocks. Actually, the Advisory began recommending the purchase and retention of precious metal issues in late 1967. We were convinced that, the approaching general bear market notwithstanding, this group would perform well.

I'm not suggesting that precious metal issues will *always* perform independently of the general market. The popular impression to that effect is also a myth. What I want to underscore, though, is that investment flexibility involves not just changing the equity ratio. It also involves the ability and willingness to recognize that at any given time, some individual stocks or groups of stocks can indeed have a life of their own.

Note further that one of the other Advisory recommendations quoted earlier advised investors to invest 20% of their funds in long-term bonds. Actually, the Recommended Investment Strategy of the Advisory always covers the entire 100% of one's investment capital. It reflects my belief that money not invested in the stock market must still be put to productive work at all times via a variety of investment vehicles. This is another integral part of the Total Investment Approach.

I might add in this regard that during the greater part of that sharp 1969-70 market break, we advised investors to allocate much of their otherwise idle funds to such short-term paper as Treasury Bills and commercial paper. Those investments not only served to protect capital, but provided investors with current income of close to 9%—a rate nearly double the typical savings-bank return.

During the second phase of the primary bear market which brought the Dow Jones industrials to below 600 by late 1974, the Advisory also recommended that investors apply some capital to selling short. Short selling is normally quite risky. But in the right environment, it can be deployed as a conservative capital-building approach. The art of selling short will also be discussed in greater detail later. To use unconventional approaches to build capital when the risk involved is limited is another example of flexibility.

CHAPTER 10

Proof of the Pudding

ADJUSTING THE PORTFOLIO COMPOSITION to minimize risk exposure on the one hand and to maximize profit potential on the other is easier said than done. Results of recent years have certainly shown that investors cannot rely on conventional Wall Street experts to help them time such adjustments. If anything, very often they'd be better off doing the very opposite of what the professionals advise.

But to follow the contrary opinion theory blindly can also be costly. Although trend-followers are wrong at major turning points, they are right when the prevailing trend persists. Back in the 1940's and the 1950's, therefore, even though the professionals as well as the masses were overwhelmingly bullish, the market nevertheless pushed ahead. Anyone who took a bearish position then just because the majority was bullish would have missed the most dynamic part of that glorious bull market.

Taking a minority position because you think the market or certain stocks are overpriced (or underpriced) can also be nerve-wracking. If your independent judgment results in an early profit, fine. But should it go against you for any length of time, the anxiety resulting from taking a minority position is alone enough to take all the fun out of investing.

To really know when to follow and not follow the crowd, and to be perfectly at ease with whichever position you take even if things go against you for a while—you must know exactly why you are doing what you are doing. Only then can you know where you went wrong if you go wrong, and make whatever adjustments are necessary in your analysis. Only then can you have full faith in your judgment.

To be fully convinced of the soundness of your judgment, you must know what makes the market behave the way it does. You must understand that knowledge can be acquired only through experience and hard work. It involves a thorough grasp of how the market has performed in the past and *why,* and what it will probably do in the foreseeable future and *why.*

This is where my Flow-of-Funds approach becomes essential.

Before I elaborate, let me first establish the soundness of this approach by citing the Advisory's record of calling the market over the past eight erratic years. So many money-making techniques have been hawked by promoters on the basis of retroactively created results that I think it would be a refreshing change for readers of this book to know beforehand how this Flow-of-Funds approach has actually fared on the firing line.

To avoid any possible criticism that I may have paraphrased statements out of context, I shall quote directly from The Holt Investment Advisory. Remember, the Advisory's judgment of the market at any given time was (and still is) expressed quantitatively in the recommended portfolio composition—the equity position in particular—and in the specific securities recommended for purchase or sale.

As I pointed out in the last chapter, we were quite bullish in the spring of 1967, when our company was formed. The May 19, 1967 issue of the Advisory stated:

> While speculation is undoubtedly present in some quarters, there is as yet no public participation . . . We therefore continue to believe that the underlying market uptrend may yet bring on a full-fledged speculative spree, participated in by the general public and centered on the glamour growth issues, special situations and well-known blue chips.

That speculative binge did come. By late September 1967, the Dow Jones industrial average was close to 950. The October 6th issue of the Advisory cautioned:

> Our analysis of the stock market, the economy and the monetary system all show that the risk of a significant market decline developing in the coming months is mounting rapidly.

In the following months, the market did retreat. By the spring of the following year, the Dow average was back to the low 800's.

Then, on April Fool's Day 1968, President Johnson surprised the nation by announcing dramatic moves to secure peace in Southeast Asia. The market responded by advancing during the remainder of the year, lifting the Dow to nearly 1000 that December. Wall Street was all set to celebrate the "imminent" topping of that magic level. But the December 20, 1968 Advisory stated:

> The Fed's belated decision to tighten credit, coupled with the delayed effect of the tax surcharge, seems almost certain to result in a business slowdown throughout 1969. The stock market, having been buoyed by easy credit and pronounced euphoria of late, is thus highly vulnerable to a major setback.

That major setback, of course, did arrive almost immediately thereafter. It lasted for about one and a half years, much longer than most Wall Streeters were prepared for. Every time a technical rally occurred during those 18 months, brokers would hail it as the start of a major recovery. But our Flow-of-Funds study helped us to keep our clients substantially out of the stock market, except to take advantage of one interim advance of fairly substantial magnitude.

In the summer of 1969, the Dow had dropped nearly 200 points to around 800. The August 15th issue of the Advisory noted:

> A drastic change in the market's technical position has taken place. We now foresee a substantial recovery starting within the next few weeks . . . We believe the forthcoming recovery, once started, will last a few months.

Three months later, in November, the Dow was back in the upper 800's, and many individual stocks had regained 25% or more. The November 21, 1969 Advisory then reminded its readers:

> Since mid-August . . . we have consistently pointed out that a primary bear market was still in progress and that the relatively more aggressive stance [we have recommended] was taken simply to capitalize on the ongoing technical rally . . . the market has now turned technically weak. The rally that started in early August will therefore probably end very soon, if it hasn't already done so.

In the six months that followed, the market pointed downward with hardly any measurable interruption. But right after the Dow Jones industrials had dropped to the low 600's in late May 1970, stock prices began a sharp upturn. The May 1, 1970 Advisory stated:

> This is it! In all probability, the market has seen its low for the year . . . The recovery in prospect will probably be far more substantial than the interim rallies of 1969.

We were wrong; the market continued to slip. The May 15th issue of the Advisory confessed:

> Oops! We goofed! We called the market bottom prematurely three weeks ago . . . But aside from exposing our fallibility potential, the market has presented subscribers with an extra opportunity to pick up stocks at bargain prices . . . With stock prices so much more attractive than they were just a few weeks ago, investors should prepare to further increase their equity holdings a few weeks from now.

As noted earlier, the market began its long recovery in late May. But for a change, Wall Street didn't believe it. The June 6, 1970 Advisory, however, recommended:

> The unexpected market tumble in May provided subscribers with an opportunity to buy stocks at extra bargain prices. The recovery in the past week alone has substantially recouped the May decline; but we think additional bargain-hunting is still warranted.

From mid-1970 to May of 1971, the market climbed from the low 600's to the mid-900's. The May 7, 1971 Advisory then forewarned:

> There is little doubt in our mind that in the months ahead the mutual fund industry will face net redemption for the first time in its history . . . Considering that the market rise of recent months has, in part, been created by concentrated buying by the funds, we think it's reasonable

> to assume that wholesale liquidation by these funds, combined with continued selling by private individuals, will result in one of the steepest drops in market history.

Less than two months later, the Investment Company Institute reported that the mutual fund industry suffered net redemptions for the first time. Wall Street was shocked. By November, the Dow Jones industrials had dropped over 150 points to below 800.

Right after Thanksgiving 1971, though, blue chip and glamour stocks suddenly took off, even though the general list continued to languish. This resulted in the so-called two-tier market, with institutional favorites selling at far loftier prices than the rest of the market. This unusual development was something we did not foresee. In fact, we had just started to incorporate short-selling as a part of the Total Investment Approach.

But our Flow-of-Funds analysis kept us from panicking. We soon discovered the reason for the two-tier market. By the following Thanksgiving, the Dow Jones industrials succeeded in topping 1000. Wall Streeters were predicting 1,500 or higher, and soon. The December 1, 1972 Advisory stated:

> Popular averages have zoomed to all-time highs; but two out of every three listed stocks and an even larger proportion of over-the-counter issues have declined since last winter . . . This dichotomy has been explained at least in part by the continuing liquidation of *all* stocks by private investors on the one hand, and the concentration of institutional purchases in just the blue-chips on the other . . . Once their purchases can no longer support stock prices, the trust officers will probably decide to suspend all new purchases, though they are likely to retain existing holdings. But since this year's strength of the blue-chips has come, quite substantially, from concentrated buying by the bank trust departments, the withdrawal of such support alone will almost certain intensify the eventual deep correction that awaits these issues.

The deep correction began shortly thereafter. This installment of the bear market lasted even longer than the first—nearly two full years. During the first year or so, stock brokers once again repeatedly predicted that a sustained recovery was just ahead. In the summer of 1973, for instance, a spirited bear market rally got underway. The Dow average climbed over 10% between August and early fall. Again, the popular glamours outpaced the general list. Euphoria returned to Wall Street. The October 5, 1973 Advisory explained:

> The support [for select glamours in recent weeks] has come from those officials running state and local government employee retirement systems . . . but underlying Flow-of-Funds trends reveal that the monies available for this purpose will soon be harder and harder to come by. Moreover, as investment losses mount, the September love affairs between the fund's supervisors and common stocks will suddenly vanish. With less support from this group, the next phase of the primary bear market may become far more damaging than the decline so far.

It was. In less than six weeks, the Dow Jones industrials lost some 200 points, sinking below 800 in early December 1973. Encouraged by the traditional yearend rally, brokers started 1974 full of enthusiasm again. But in its predictions for 1974, the January 4, 1974 Advisory stated:

> By mid-year, we predict, *even triple-A rated [bond] issues will have to offer 10% interest* or higher . . . Annual interest of 10% or more on high-grade bonds cannot help but draw still more funds from the equity market. Even institutional investors will decide that investing in bonds is more rewarding and less risky. Thus, the underlying trend for stocks will continue to point downward. We predict that *at its low, the Dow Jones industrial average will be in the 500's.*

Ironically, when the Dow Jones industrials did sink into the upper 500's in the fall of 1974, the perennially bullish brokers and money managers at the big banks were too scared to buy bargains. They were panic-stricken.

Just before the final break came, the September 6th Advisory published an analysis titled "Call Us Superbull" with the following conclusion:

> Summing up, the market has, in recent months, undergone a perfect classic collapse. It has resulted mainly from intense liquidation by under-margined accounts and panicky professionals. This wave of involuntary and emotional selling will be over soon. Thereafter, renewed acquisitions by serious investors as well as financial institutions will bring about one of the sharpest bear market rallies in recent history.

That sharp rally did arrive shortly thereafter, and by mid-1975 the Dow Jones industrials were over 875 again.

The record of The Holt Investment Advisory was not perfect. But it's probably a lot better than that of most Wall Street experts. More important, it does reveal an understanding on our part of why the market went up and down. And it testifies to the fact that the Flow-of-Funds approach *is* effective.

CHAPTER 11

A Simple Case of Supply and Demand

LESS THAN MODEST though it is, the I-told-you-so presentation in the last two chapters is meant to convince you that I have not been just lucky. The published record proves that the Flow-of-Funds approach does work. It is not a gimmick; not a magic formula; not even a new theory. It works simply because it combines common sense and knowledge with the most elementary law of economics.

To help you better understand what it is all about, let me explain how I use the Flow-of-Funds study to analyze the stock market. Its basic concept applies, however, to other markets as well.

A market is a "place" where sellers and buyers meet together to trade. In a free market, the price of anything so traded is determined by the relationship between the money the buyer is willing and able to pay and the money the seller is willing and able to take out. In short, it is governed by the money inflow versus the outflow. This is a simple and direct measure of supply and demand. The most fundamental of all economic laws, it is indisputable.

Applying this basic supply-and-demand law to stock market analysis, I first study how much money has been put into the market by various groups of investors, and how much has been taken out by others. To do so, I first separate the factors affecting such flow into four prime classifications: Private Individuals, Institutional Investors, Corporations, and Others, which include banks and foreign investors.

To refine my analysis, I then subdivide these four classifications into over 20 smaller groups. These are groups for which I can obtain reliable statistics and/or make reasonable estimates. Some of the more popularly known are:

1) Mutual funds
2) Market specialists
3) Margin traders
4) Odd-lot investors
5) Insurance companies
6) Pension funds
7) Finance companies
8) Corporate insiders
9) State and local government retirement funds
10) Stock exchange members
11) Floor traders
12) Real estate investment trusts

By analyzing the flow of money controlled by these groups in the past and correlating the flow to the concurrent market movement, it is possible to understand roughly why stock prices have moved up and down and, more importantly, whose buying and whose selling was *primarily* responsible for the move at any given time.

Next, the economic, monetary and other developments that unfolded in the period under study are reviewed to determine what might have motivated the various groups of investors to do whatever they did. I also analyze the amount of new investment capital received by those groups to determine how the availability of funds, or the lack thereof, might have affected their buying and selling patterns.

Then I find out what economic picture is most widely accepted at present. This gives me some idea as to what those investing groups who typically respond to the standard forecast are currently doing in the market. (Later in this book, I shall explain why the so-called standard forecast is frequently wrong.)

An *independent* study of the economic and monetary prospects is then made. It's important to know how the various groups of investors are likely to react when economic and monetary prospects actually materialize, as well as how much new savings will be generated and how much new equity capital corporations will have to raise.

Adding a little imagination to the results from these research studies, I then estimate how much money the various groups are expected to put into or withdraw from the stock market. Finally, all those estimates are put together to find out whether a net inflow or a net outflow is indicated for the period under study.

If the total inflow exceeds the total outflow, demand exceeds supply and a rising market is ahead. If the total outflow exceeds the inflow, on the other hand, a down market can be expected. It's as simple as that.

But the Flow-of-Funds study does not just indicate whether the market will go up or down; it does much more. For instance, the magnitude of the imbalance between the prospective inflow and outflow of funds indicates the probable steepness of the coming market trend.

Back in late 1972, I delivered a speech to a group of investors at the Waldorf Astoria in New York City. In that address, I discussed the Flow of Funds on the basis of the four major classifications I mentioned earlier. Using the indicated flow in 1972 as a reference point, I then presented two sets of estimates for 1973: conservative figures made on admittedly optimistic assumptions, and projections that I considered to be more probable. My conclusion:

> For 1973, even my conservative estimates for the three groups show a balance of minus $13 billion. And the more probable estimates show a shortage of some $29 billion. It only takes a gap of a few billion dollars in supply and demand pressure to bring on a substantial market drop . . . Prepare for a sizeable market decline in 1973.

The theme of that speech was published several weeks later by *Business Week,* which also quoted my prediction of "below 600" for the Dow Jones industrial average. Coincidentally, that address was delivered on Friday, December 8, 1972. The following Monday, December 11, 1972, the Dow Jones industrial registered its all-time closing high—a high which I believe will stand for at least a decade. (This is where luck came in!)

By the nature of its analytical process, the Flow-of-Funds study also automatically identifies the investor groups who are likely to be especially heavy buyers in the near future and those who are likely to be heavy sellers. This added information is significant because it helps anticipate the relative strength of major stock groups.

For instance, in that same Waldorf Astoria address, I pointed out that between 1972 and 1973, by far the most dramatic change in the flow pattern would come from those traders who bought stocks on credit. In 1972, total security debt, including loans extended by banks as well as brokers, more than doubled to a record high. That jump came even though private investors as a whole had been selling stocks quite heavily on balance. I observed:

> While serious investors own hundreds of billions of dollars worth of stocks which they can sell, the amount of money margined speculators can put into the market is limited. In 1971 and 1972, the equity they have to put up already totalled over $12 billion. And that's a very large figure. Even the entire pension fund industry didn't have that much money to put into the [stock] market. So, it's safe to assume that there won't be any increase in margin debt next year.

I went on to explain that instead of standing pat, chances were margin traders would have to liquidate stocks quite heavily in 1973 to pay off their loans. Thus, a major inflow factor in 1972 was changing into a formidable outflow factor.

Since margin-using traders typically buy volatile and speculative stocks, epitomized by those traded on the American Stock Exchange, the inference was drawn that stocks listed on that junior exchange would be subject to especially heavy selling. That was precisely what happened.

This feature of the Flow-of-Funds study is equally valuable in spotting stocks that are coming into favor. In the October 18, 1974 issue of The Holt Investment Advisory, we advised investors to start buying electric utility stocks in a big way. Aside from my belief that the industry's problems were gradually easing, we noted that the developing market recovery would be triggered by heavy bargain-hunting by private, long-term investors.

Inasmuch as private investors are not generally concerned over the immediate prospects for the economy, we reasoned the then approaching business contraction would not bother them. Moreover, past studies showed that they prefer conservative issues that provide good income.

Since electric utilities are generally regarded as conservative issues and since many were then yielding up to 14%-15%, an increase in the demand for these stocks was indicated. Significantly, utility shares did lead the general market recovery in late 1974. The Dow Jones utility index bottomed out in September, three months ahead of the industrials.

As I pointed out earlier in this chapter, the concept behind the Flow-of-Funds approach—measuring supply and demand to anticipate price trends—is by no means applicable only to the stock market. I have also found it very helpful in analyzing gold and gold shares, too.

Many Wall Street observers classify me as a "gold bug." That's probably because I have always publicly stated my strong belief in hard money and sound government fiscal policies. I've always maintained that when politicians create fiat money to win votes, the unsuspecting public foots the bill in the end. A monetary system disciplined by gold is one way to help minimize abuses by demagogic government leaders.

But like personal emotion, economic and political philosophy and timely investment programs are not always compatible. Until the late 1960's, I did not foresee any unusual influx of funds into the gold market.

In November 1967, however, the Bank of England suddenly devalued the pound sterling. As the sterling was then one of the two primary reserve currencies, I reasoned that devaluation could not help but induce an increasing flow of funds into the gold market. Eleven days later, therefore, The Holt Investment Advisory sent out a Special Bulletin advising investors to start buying gold shares in a big way.

Notwithstanding the U.S. Treasury's repeated efforts to belittle gold, notwithstanding central bankers' earlier attempts to keep the old $35 official price intact, and notwithstanding the many liberal press campaigns to depress the free-market quotation, my firm has helped investors ride the gold price uptrend throughout the last several years, because my analysis has consistently revealed that there has been a net inflow of investment money into both the gold bullion and the gold stock markets.

I have also used the Flow-of-Funds approach to analyze the bond market. Here, the analytical process is somewhat simpler. The inflow of funds is generally represented by new savings, while the outflow of funds is accounted for by the sale of new bonds by corporations and by the federal, state and local governments. Liquidation of outstanding issues by bondholders is a relatively minor factor.

In early 1974, readers may recall, economists and businessmen alike were all looking toward a booming year ahead. Capital expenditures by utilities and manufacturers alike were expected to soar, keeping the economy bubbling in the process.

Nevertheless, in a speech I delivered on January 19th in New Orleans before the Monetary Symposium sponsored by The National Committee to Legalize Gold, I discussed the Flow-of-Funds relating to the bond market, and concluded:

> Putting all these factors together and even allowing for a further decline in housing starts, I think the demand for long-term capital in 1974 will exceed the available supply by perhaps $75 billion.
>
> The upshot of this imbalance is that later this year, free-market forces will act to close the gap. First, interest rates will rise sharply. Even triple A bonds will carry coupons of well over 10%. This will encourage increased personal saving. The resultant decline in consumer spending will cause retail sales to plunge . . .
>
> We will also suddenly see a widespread cutback of capital spending plans. Most of those bulging unfilled orders of capital goods now outstanding are thus illusory.

As subsequent developments proved, this Flow-of-Funds study not only helped keep investors from getting caught in the 1974 bond market collapse, it also came up with a rather good economic forecast.

CHAPTER 12

Always Room for Improvements

YOU ARE PROBABLY THINKING at this point that while its concept is simple, the Flow-of-Funds approach is really quite demanding in its implementation. You are right. It involves a good deal of research—not only of the stock market, but of the economy at home and abroad as well. It also requires imagination, independent thinking, and an understanding of human psychology.

But then, investment success is never easy to achieve.

Notice, though, that this approach to analyzing the stock market is logical. That alone is more than any conventional method can claim. By way of contrast, such typical Wall Street statements as "Stocks should keep climbing because the economy is pulling out of the recession," or "The drop in interest rates will result in a bull market," or "A sharp tumble is ahead because the market has just completed a head-and-shoulder formation" are all *non-sequiturs*. Based mainly on unsupported theories and devoid of logic, these statements in my opinion insult the intelligence of rational investors.

The Flow-of-Funds approach is also flexible. It does not tolerate such rigid views as "Big money means smart money," or "Corporate insiders are the ones to follow," or "Odd-lotters are usually wrong." Nor does it accept such rules of thumb as "A higher money-supply growth rate means higher price/earnings ratios" or "The market must go up in an election year." Instead, it gives weight to various investor groups and various external factors only in accordance with their impact on the overall flow picture.

The only principle to which it adheres rigidly and faithfully is that changing stock prices result from a changing relationship between supply and demand; and that relationship can be quantified by the amounts of funds flowing into and out of the market.

The Flow-of-Funds approach recognizes the supreme importance of good independent economic research. But it also takes into consideration the standard forecasts. It utilizes these business forecasts flexibly to find out how the economy has been affected and how it will affect the investing pattern of the various investor groups.

Similarly, the Flow-of-Funds study appreciates the need for good monetary and technical analyses. But here again, no stock market judgment is directly drawn from those studies. They are conducted to help determine how the supply and demand situation in the stock market may be influenced.

Let us now apply Flow-of Funds study retroactively to see how it explains the market behavior of the past.

During the Forties, Fifties and the early part of the Sixties, almost all major groups of investors—old-line institutions, mutual funds, foreign investors, the general public, etc.—put money into the stock market. Only corporations, through the offering of new shares, regularly took money out; and the amounts involved were relatively small. As a result, the market just had to trend upward—rising earnings multiples, shrinking dividend yields, and intervening recessions notwithstanding.

When that bull market first started in the 1940's, most of the big buyers were wealthy individuals who had witnessed the 1929 crash and the Great Depression. They therefore concentrated their purchases mostly on the old-line blue chips. That's why a staid average like the Dow-Jones industrials was among the first to turn upward.

By way of contrast, when the bull market was in its final stages in 1967-68, just about everyone with some money to spare was speculating in the market. Thus, while billions of investment dollars were being removed by serious investors, even more billions of speculating dollars were poured into the market by newcomers. Naive and gullible, few of the new breed had any conception of a real bear market. They bought every stock touted by brokers. This explains why during those years the Dow industrials moved sluggishly while little-known stocks traded on the American Stock Exchange and over-the-counter catapulted.

The quarter-century primary bull market was actually composed of many interim advances and declines of substantial magnitudes. Long-term investors seldom change their investment patterns markedly from one year to another. The secondary movements were therefore generated mainly by the flow of those funds connected with the relatively more active and more sophisticated investors and with fund-raising corporations.

Sophisticated investors, be they individuals or institutions, are typically quite economy-oriented. They follow business developments closely, buying or selling stocks on the basis of their expectations of corporation earnings. Generally, the more astute succeed in getting out of the market long before a recession arrives; the less sophisticated bail out only after bad economic news has made the headlines. In both cases, however, their flow of funds corresponds to the business cycle.

Corporate need for new capital also ties in closely with the business swing. When the economy emerges from a recession, most businesses have ample working capital and plant capacity. But toward the end of a boom, the need grows for additional capital to carry inventories and accounts receivable and to help finance capital expansion programs. Hence the number of new equity offerings increases.

For these reasons, the *secondary* advances and declines within a *primary* market tend to correlate to the economic cycle. They often lead by six to nine months. It is this phenomenon that has misled many observers into believing that successful investment can be attained by just correctly anticipating business cycles and making good earnings estimates. And it is this correlation that has prompted economists to regard the market as a leading indicator.

Actually, relative to the overall size of the market, the amount of money controlled by sophisticated investors is quite small. And only once in a long while are new equity offerings by corporations a significant factor. The fact is, until the early 1970's, new corporate issues seldom exceeded $2 billion a year. Other than in a handful of major cities, newspapers seldom carry more than one or two columns of business and financial news. So-called sophisticated investors, therefore, are usually active traders and businessmen who read the *Wall Street Journal,* or investors who live near major metropolitan areas.

By way of contrast, serious investors—the "silent majority" of the stock market—still directly own over two-thirds of all corporate shares outstanding, as well as an overwhelming proportion of all liquid financial assets. These investors, unlike financial institutions, don't turn over their portfolios actively. But because of their collective size, the flow of their capital more often than not determines the underlying market tide.

Our Flow-of-Funds analysis thus shows that the interim movements within a primary bull or bear market are analogous to the surface waves on top of a rising or ebbing ocean tide—a tide that most people simply take for granted.

In the early 1960's, those forgotten private investors began selling stocks on balance. In other words, they started withdrawing funds from the equity market.

Why did they do so at a time when the economy was growing robustly and when there was no interference from Vietnam, Watergate, the fuel crisis, or whatever? It's because this group is overwhelmingly income-oriented.

Back in the Forties, common stocks were yielding far more than bonds. Those lush yields dropped as stock prices rose. By the late Fifties, stock yields began to fall below bond yields. But the market's upward momentum was so strong that these investors were willing to stay put.

In early 1962, the market underwent a sharp nosedive for no apparent reason. Though stock prices subsequently recovered, that break was sufficient to remind serious investors that growth could no longer be taken for granted to make up for the rapidly declining stock yields. They started turning to higher-income investment media instead.

For a few years, funds withdrawn by serious individuals were fully offset by the inflow of institutional and speculating money. But as selling by individuals increased in the late 1960's, the scale tipped the other way. Stock prices began to weaken in early 1969. That in turn triggered more public disillusionment and public selling. Together with heavy offerings by corporations, the withdrawal of funds by the silent majority finally put an end to the primary bull market by yearend 1968 and triggered the 1969-70 bear market that followed.

Although public liquidation remained heavy in 1971-72, fund managers resumed pouring billions of dollars of institutional money into the market. But this time, the professionals concentrated much of their buying on a select group of blue chips and glamours. This accounted for the renewed strength of the big-name issues in the early Seventies and the emergence of the two-tier market.

As I explained earlier, a dramatic swing in the funds controlled by margin-using traders turned the market downward again in 1973. That year, while secondary and volatile stocks were particularly hard hit, the upper-tier stocks held up relatively well. By early 1974, as a result, they became conspicuously overpriced in relation to the general list. Free-market forces then entered to close the gap.

In the spring and summer of 1974, public liquidation of those upper-tier, low-yield issues became exceptionally heavy. The amount offered soon became far too much for the financial institutions to absorb. The crumbling of the upper-tier stocks was thus inevitable.

The summer collapse of 1974 was so sharp and scary that by autumn most traders had either fully withdrawn their funds from the market or had resigned themselves to the fact that their bad investments were worth too little to sell. Institutional investors, too, had been stunned into suspending most of their buying programs, putting idle cash into short-term paper instead. Meanwhile, the demoralized market resulted in a near total absence of new corporate offerings.

With the outflow of funds having thus contracted, the way was paved for the subsequent inflow of money from bargain-hunting investors that would trigger the sharp recovery of December 1974. Not surprisingly, once institutions began pumping idle funds back into the stock market, a mini two-tier market emerged in the first half of 1975.

For all its merits, the Flow-of-Funds approach is not infallible. Its reliability depends a good deal on the ability to correctly forecast economic, monetary and even social developments, the ability to figure out how these developments influence the buying and selling of the various investor groups, and the ability to make sound assumptions about the future money flow.

Moreover, unexpected developments can very often throw original assumptions off. For that reason, it is necessary to regularly update assumptions and estimates. With the help of new input, erasing major flaws becomes an almost automatic process.

For instance, you may recall that my firm had just started selling short for clients in early 1972 when the institutional favorites suddenly surged upward. My Flow-of-Funds study had not assumed that the trust departments of big banks would pour so much of the money they controlled into a handful of favorite issues.

Nevertheless, because the Flow-of-Funds analysis was based on clearly defined assumptions, it was not too difficult to find out what went wrong. Once it became clear that professional money managers were supporting their favorite stocks, I made a special study to determine how much longer they could play that game.

Specifically, I analyzed the trend of new money going into the pension and retirement funds and the trend of payments made by these funds to participating pensioners. Matching the maximum amount of money the bank managers can inject into the "Favorite Fifty" and the probable amount of money private investors would take out from the sale of those same stocks, it became clear that the glamour stocks could not be held up much beyond

1972. So, instead of covering shorts in panic, we increased our clients' short positions with new conviction. Those shorts, of course, resulted in handsome profits by the fall of 1974.

What these examples show is that, by being flexible and open-minded and by constantly updating the analysis with fresh information, the Flow-of-Funds approach, though not infallible, has indeed been more effective in correctly anticipating the market than, to my knowledge, any other approach available.

CHAPTER 13

If You Were an Economist

AFTER HAVING READ the last couple of chapters, you probably understand why I consider an accurate appraisal of the business prospect to be absolutely essential to successful investing—even though economic analysis, by itself, does not directly predict what the market will do.

In a nutshell, not everyone buys or sells stocks on the basis of how many automobiles are sold or by what percentage corporate profits rise. But every single investor is an integral part of the economy. One way or another, business conditions affect his welfare and finances, and influence his decision to buy or sell stocks.

Unfortunately, getting a realistic appraisal of the economy is where most investors run into trouble.

Like investment experts, economists are excellent forecasters when things are moving smoothly according to well established trends or following typical paths of the past. But once conditions depart a bit from the norm, they are no better than the man on the street.

Worse yet, this profession seems to come right out of Alice's wonderland. Often, the more damaging the mistakes an economist makes, the more respected he becomes. That makes it especially hard for the lay investor to know whom to turn to.

Today, the most responsible and respected economist in the country, according to a public opinion poll, is Chairman Arthur Burns of the Federal Reserve Board. When testifying before Congressional committees, Administration spokesmen are usually severely cross-examined, if not tongue-lashed, by headline-hunting lawmakers. Not so with Mr. Burns. When he speaks, everyone listens attentively. Even the usually critical press reports his statements with deference.

The pipe-smoking FRB Chairman does project an image of statesmanship. And what he preaches usually makes good sense. To illustrate, this is what he said in a speech made in Los Angeles:

> The broad thrust of monetary policy during the past few years has been more and more expansionist. . . . It is this combination of an accelerating growth of the money supply and an increasingly expansionist fiscal policy that is the basic cause of the wage-price spiral that we have lately been experiencing. . . . Now, as in other times of inflation, the Administration in power has been blaming greedy businessmen, irresponsible trade union leaders and unruly Congressmen. But the new inflation mainly is the result of the excessively rapid creation of new money and of our unbalanced federal budgets.

How much more objective could any economist get? And how right he was about inflation! But wait! The passage above was taken from a speech Burns *preached* in May 1968, nearly two years before he became the Fed's Chairman.

Let's see what he *practiced* after he was put into a position in early 1969 to shape the nation's monetary policy. The money supply has since increased at an accelerating rate. From time to time in the last few years the Fed has been accused of keeping its grip on credit too tightly. But it is undisputable that under Dr. Burns' aegis, the FRB has permitted the money supply to grow at an annual rate of 6.3%, some 75% *faster* than the average 3.6% annual rate of the preceding quarter century.

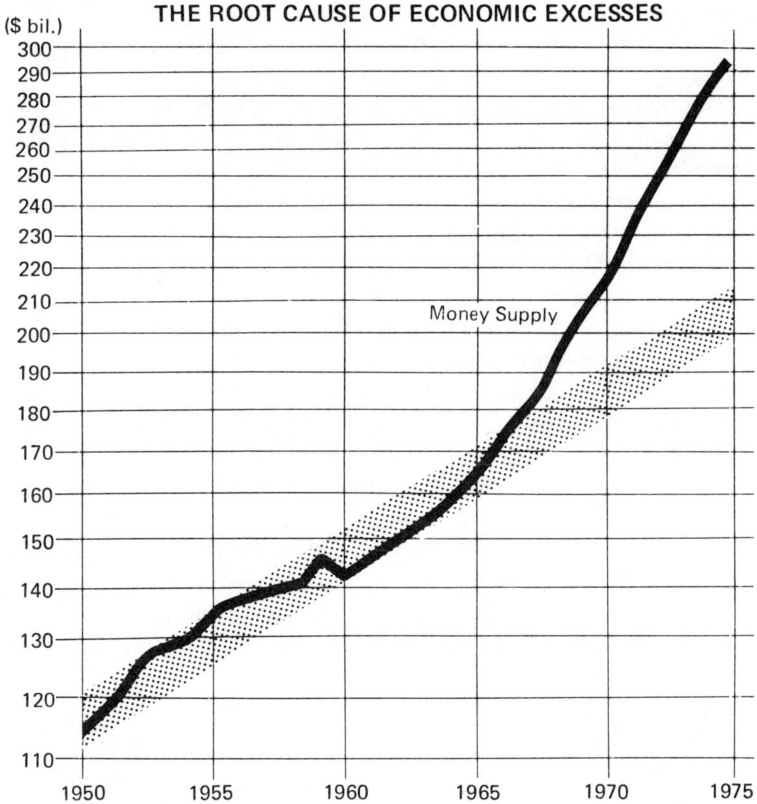

The U.S. money supply—currency plus checking account deposits—has been inflated by the Federal Reserve Board's liberal monetary policy. It has risen at a much faster pace than the nation's real economic growth in the past decade. The excesses have been particularly pronounced since 1969, when Arthur Burns became the Fed's chairman.

The U.S. Treasury is supposed to be independent of the Federal Reserve Board. But it cannot really raise much money without the Fed's helping hand. In the past five years, the Federal fiscal deficits have totaled over $110 billion, compared with $37 billion in the preceding five years.

The facts thus reveal that the venerable Mr. Burns, by sanctioning rapid money growth and staggering fiscal deficits, is the single person most responsible by far for the double digit inflation of recent years. That dislocation, of course, triggered the business contraction now besetting the entire free world.

Not surprisingly, Mr. Arthur Burns was also the very first monetary leader to recommend the wage and price controls which President Nixon subsequently implemented. That "incomes policy" was no doubt the biggest economic blunder the government has made in modern history.

Second to Dr. Burns in popularity among economists, according to the same public opinion survey, is Mr. Alan Greenspan, Chairman of the President's Council of Economic Advisors. He, too, has gained unusual respect from the financial press and lawmakers on both sides of the aisle. One of the not-so-liberal economists to assume that post, he is supposed to be more realistic than most of his predecessors.

But Mr. Greenspan was certainly less than realistic when he gave President Ford his first major advice. At a time when free-market forces were already slowing inflation and were ushering in the worst business slump since the Depression, the President declared in late summer 1974 that "there will be no recession" and proceeded, instead, to launch his ill-fated "Whip Inflation Now" program.

After the "surprising" nosedive in retail sales that fall, Mr. Greenspan discovered that a recession was in progress. He insisted, however, that the contraction would be so mild that the unemployment rate would not go above 7%. Subsequently, however, he quietly revised the peak unemployment rate he thought probable about half a percentage point every month.

Actually, inaccuracy in government economic forecasts is endemic. In modern history, not once has the federal budget ended up anywhere near the figures originally projected.

The trouble with these economists is that they function on the wrong premise to start with; they believe that a bureaucratic government can control the free economy.

Let's not get bogged down debating the point. Just look at the economy at home and abroad. Despite management by one government after another, hundreds of millions of people are now having trouble making ends meet. The implications are clear: 1) bureaucrats cannot really manage the economy, and 2) they do such a terrible job trying that the economy would be much better off without their interference.

Government economists are especially unreliable when things go wrong. They somehow think they must feed the public optimistic forecasts. Their reason: the American public is too timid to face up to realities, so any official projection that is less than rosy would result in panic.

If government economists are unreliable, those representing the business establishment are not much better. It's an open secret that the leaders of big banks and big business work hand in hand with the Washington planners. Therefore, they follow the same party line.

Moreover, business and banking leaders have a vested interest in keeping the public optimistic. What the realities are is not important. Only a confident consumer, they reason, will spend freely to buy homes and automobiles. Only a confident businessman will borrow unhesitatingly to accumulate inventories. Only a confident executive will push vigorously for new expansion programs.

What about the thousands of independent economists who are not connected with the government or with the financial-industrial establishment? Shouldn't they do a more credible job? Perhaps the best way to answer that question is to hypothetically make you an economist.

Let's say that you have a Ph.D in economics and have worked at your profession for a number of years. So, now you know what GNP, CPI, and IMF mean. You know that M3, M4 and M5 represent various measures of the money supply and not a series of rifles. You don't like government work, so you either teach in a college or work in the business world.

You've found that teaching is less competitive. Most of your students aren't experienced enough to effectively challenge what you tell them. So you can never be wrong. And you don't have to stick your neck out making forecasts.

But if you are more ambitious than your associates, you may

want to promote a pet theory about the economy. Whether your theory works in the real business world is immaterial. If you talk about it long enough, you will sooner or later find some believers. To that end, you do make economic forecasts, but they are designed to promote your pet theory. If those forecasts turn out to be wrong, no problem. Just blame the "jungle" outside your classroom; market forces are *supposed* to act the way your theory says they should.

Because industry often pays more than colleges, you may decide to become an economist in the business world. Instead of dealing with economic laws and theories, you now have to know something about current housing starts and steel output. At least once a year, you are required to put out a set of forecasts. How should you get that job done?

You can spend a lot of time and energy working independently to come up with your own projections. If your projections are significantly different from those published by outside sources, you may want to stand by them because you take pride in your work. If you prove to be right a year hence, you'll have great personal satisfaction. Your boss may give you a big pat on the back and a small bonus. But if you are wrong, you stand to lose your $20,000 job.

So, on second thought, you decide it's not worth it. Why not play it safe? So you take the projections circulated freely by the government and the banks, and make a few minor adjustments so that you can put your own signature on the report. One year hence, if those projections turn out right, you'll get that big pat on the back and the small bonus. If not, however, you still keep your job. After all, if the President's Council of Economic Advisors and the economists at the big banks and corporations are all wrong, your boss will reason, obviously whatever went astray was something totally unforeseeable.

The upshot of all this is that very few economists really have the incentive to be right. In our free enterprise system, competition and incentives are what create excellence. That is why, when you come right down to it, only those who are seeking investment success are truly motivated to undertake realistic economic studies. When they are wrong, the fact that other economists are also wrong will not compensate for real investment losses. When they are right, the financial rewards can run into five, six, even seven figures. These investor-economists, then, are the ones investors should rely on for business forecasts.

CHAPTER 14

One Crystal Ball Worked

ECONOMISTS SEEKING investment success should not be confused with economists associated with "successful" investment firms. Many large brokerage houses have economists as well as securities analysts in their research departments, but they are not the ones I'm talking about.

The truly motivated economist is more likely to be an entrepreneur whose fortune and reputation rests squarely on the accuracy of his economic analysis. There are not too many of them. In the last few years, several have indeed succeeded in keeping open-minded investors from getting caught in the bad market storm. Unfortunately, not all of them have been right for the right reasons.

There is, for example, an egregiously outspoken economist who writes newspaper columns and appears frequently on talk shows. He was super-bearish in the early 1970's. So, since the market underwent its nosedive in the fall of 1974, he has become ever so much more opinionated.

There is no doubt whatsoever that he did foresee the market break. The trouble is, he had been foreseeing it for decades.

Throughout those years, he used virtually every economic and political development to rationalize his preconceived position that a major stock market crash and a severe economic depression were imminent. So, as someone once said, even a broken clock gives the right time twice a day.

Moreover, ever since the stock market turned sour and the inflation rate hit the two-digit level, a new group of iconoclastic economists has come out of hibernation. In sharp contrast to the Establishment optimists, these soothsayers openly predict that the world economy and the social order are both about to collapse. For salvation, they declare, one must stock up on gold, a few years' supply of canned foods, several shotguns, and lots of ammunition.

True, these economists are entrepreneurs and their fortunes have indeed grown by virtue of their willingness to openly depart from the conventional wisdom.

But I think today's Cassandras are no better than yesterday's Pollyannas. Those who exploit people's fear in the current confusion are just as misleading as those who exploited people's greed during the bull market heydays. Economic analysis, whether optimistic or pessimistic, should always appeal to logic, not emotion.

Many of today's "survival" advisors, for instance, are predicting that the U.S. will go through a depression that is worse than that of the 1930's. There will be wholesale bank failures and widespread corporate and personal bankruptcies. Riots will flare out across the land. I personally don't expect the depression to be that bad. But at least up to this point, there is logic behind their thinking. Both the domestic and the world economies have been inflated by decades of credit expansion; a corrective period of economic contraction can hardly be avoided.

Nevertheless, these same experts are also saying that inflation will accelerate in the years ahead; prices will rise so steeply that the dollar will become virtually worthless before long. In a few years, they predict, the government will give us one new dollar in exchange for each $10, $100 or $1,000 of the present greenbacks. At this point, logic has been forgotten.

In my opinion, these observers have arbitrarily combined the miseries caused by the Great Depression here in the States with those resulting from runaway inflation in France, Germany and China one or two generations ago to form a big fear package. It gets attention. But it's short on reasoning.

The United States is quite different from the Germany, the France, or the China that was hit by runaway inflation a few generations ago. For one thing, government outlays here are large and growing, to be sure; but relative to the gross national product, they aren't nearly as large as they were in those countries. Moreover, unlike the old German mark, the old French franc and the old Chinese yen, the dollar is a reserve currency still extensively held by central banks. Finally, the U. S. economy is characterized by a highly efficient credit and capital market. It wasn't so in those countries. For these and many other reasons, it is simply impossible for a severe depression in this country to go hand in hand with runaway inflation.

In a recession, prices can indeed continue to climb. While income and output drop, total demand for goods and services can be inflated by the increasing use of debt.

But depression is not just a bad recession. It corrects for excessive debt expansion. As it unfolds, debt is reduced and total demand shrinks. At the very least, the rate of inflation drops. As and if total demand contracts faster than total supply, prices actually come down.

Typically, the deflation process begins when marginal businesses find it necessary to liquidate inventories at reduced prices to raise cash in order to pay off maturing loans, and when marginal consumers have to cut down on current purchases in order to pay off installment and mortgage debt.

That is why, in early 1975, the inflation rate surprised many people by dropping back to around 6%, even though feverish government spending during that period boosted the fiscal deficit to a record peacetime high.

It is distinctly possible, of course, for the government to go haywire and boost federal spending many, many times more. At some point, the rise in federal expenditures would then be large enough to offset the contraction in the private sector. The fiscal debt would then be so monstrous as to seriously erode the value of the dollar. But with that kind of massive spending, total debt would increase, as would total demand for goods and services. We could end up with a socialist economy and runaway inflation, but it would not be a depression worse than the Thirties.

What it boils down to is this: the United States, with some $2.5 *trillion* of private debt outstanding, is uniquely different from other countries. We can have rapid inflation, or we can have deep depression. But we cannot have both simultaneously.

At this point, you may be wondering if there are any economists who can really analyze the economy logically. Are optimistic economists only right when the economy is booming and pessimstic economists only right when the nation's business is falling?

Again, let's look at the published record of The Holt Investment Advisory. You may recall that the sharp drop in business activities toward the end of 1974 came as a total surprise to almost everyone, including President Ford and his chief economic advisor, Mr. Greeenspan. None of the many, many experts attending the economic summit meeting in Washington as late as September foresaw it. Even those perennially pessimistic economists who had predicted economic chaos for years failed to realize that a major slowdown was imminent.

Yet the January 4, 1974 issue of the Advisory included the following section pertaining to the domestic economy in its "Predictions for 1974":

> At home, the ultra-fast increase in the money supply in the past four years also means, of course, that U.S. banks, too, have loaned out their funds at an ultra-fast rate. The entire banking system is now highly illiquid . . .
>
> On the other side of the coin, bank customers—both individuals and corporations—have become dangerously illiquid as well. For many, the burden of servicing and amortizing outstanding debt is already claiming an excessive chunk of future income or profits. For many marginal borrowers, any significant decline in such income would result in insolvency . . .
>
> Rampant inflation is, of course, how free-market forces respond to excessive debt-financed demand; and widespread shortages are how they react to price controls. (The Arabian oil embargo is just a minor factor that serves to worsen a situation that had existed long before

the new Mideast conflict.) Henceforth, employment disruptions stemming from shortages and a continuing rise in the cost of staple goods and basic services (such as heating and transportation) will keep eroding the average family's *real* spendable income *and borrowing power.* As a result, we predict, *retail sales, those of durable goods in particular, will soften—gradually at first, markedly later . . .*

. . . When consumers are forced to allocate a good part of their take-home pay or unemployment checks to retire outstanding mortgage or installment debt, they obviously are in no position to incur new borrowings. The same holds true for marginal businesses. Hit by mounting bad debts, banks, too, will be less inclined to grant new loans willy-nilly. Accordingly, we predict *beginning in late 1974, total private debt will contract for the first time in decades.*

Whereas rapid debt expansion has generated greater-than-normal demand for goods and services in the last several years, the prospective debt liquidation will result in lower-than-normal demand. Ironically, this sharp swing from one extreme to another will come at a time when manufacturers are still responding to the recent boom by feverishly boosting output. The supply and demand balance will be suddenly thrown out of kilter. Since many business outfits are confronted with the need to pay off bank borrowings, we predict that *there will be widespread price cutting toward the end of 1974* as manufacturers and retailers try to liquidate excessive inventories to raise cash.

What we envision then is that a year from now, the nation—instead of worrying about inflation and shortages—will witness a general price decline and excessive inventories. *This sudden turn of events, we submit, will be the single 1974 development that will hit most Americans as a total surprise.*

It's quite apparent that few business leaders, if any, are entertaining any thought of deflation. In the early months of 1974, they will keep on building new plants and equipment. What they do not realize is that there's no way the capital market can possibly accommodate their financing needs.

Businesses generate their internal cash flow from retained earnings and depreciation. The latter is based on the original cost of plant and equipment. Because of the recent inflationary spiral, the cost of replacing an old plant has skyrocketed. As a result, most firms have found that internally generated funds are grossly inadequate to meet current capital needs. To make up the difference, they have had to undertake increasing external financing . . .

. . . Even so, many individual firms won't be able to obtain the money they need. By the second half, their ambitious capital expansion projects will have to be drastically trimmed or shelved. Other firms will be unable to retire bank loans that are coming due, going into receivership as a result. We therefore predict that, contrary to current expectations, *capital outlays in the second half will be lower than in the first half.*

Note from the above that the predictions made at the very start of 1974 did not all come true. Toward the very end of the year, consumers did begin to pay off installment debt on balance for the first time in the post-World War II era. But business loans did not begin to show a net reduction until the start of 1975. And as of this writing, mortgage debt was still showing net increases, though the rate of increase was shrinking.

Note also that there wasn't any widespread price cutting toward the end of 1974. It was only in early 1975 that automobile and appliance manufacturers began to make "rebate" a household word. Similarly, business capital expenditures began to drop only in the first quarter of 1975.

Note, however, that all the predictions made were supported by logic. So, where the Advisory was wrong, it was mostly a matter of timing. Where it was right—about retail sales softening at first and then weakening sharply thereafter, about corporations failing to find adequate outside capital, about real estate prices depressed by the bad-debt problem, about bank failures—it was right for the right reasons.

The conclusion, then, is that reasonably reliable economic forecasts can indeed be made. It involves recognizing the major underlying forces and applying common sense to predict probable changes. With this kind of rational analysis, the 180° turn taken by President Ford less than two months after launching the much ballyhooed Whip Inflation Now program would never have been necessary.

CHAPTER 15

And Now, the Bad News

SO MUCH FOR THE PAST. Now let's see how one can best protect and build capital in the years ahead. To do so, of course, we must first try to envision what economic climate we can reasonably anticipate.

Unlike the economic analysis in the twice-a-month Holt Advisory, I shall discuss only the longer-term economic trend in this book. Business inventories, housing starts, capital appropriations and the like change directions so frequently that current discussions regarding short-term or even intermediate-term economic developments may well be out of date by the time you read this book.

Let me emphasize right at the outset that within the long-term scenario I now foresee, there will inevitably be counter-moves of considerable magnitude and duration in both the economy and the investment market. Many capital-building opportunities will be presented by such interim moves. But to avoid confusion and to simplify an otherwise complex subject, this discussion will not cover them. I'll concentrate on identifying only the underlying tide.

Moreover, as new information becomes available in the months and years ahead, my views of the future will inevitably be modified. This is part of being flexible. My comments will thus be based strictly on evidence now at hand.

To figure out what the economy will probably do in the years ahead, let's first review briefly what it has done in the past, and—more importantly—find out why. This should help us determine objectively whether past trends are likely to be extended, moderated, or reversed.

Until recently, the world economy had undergone decades of unprecedented growth. The reconstruction of Japan and the Western European countries has been all but miraculous. Devastated by the Second World War, many of these nations have since become industrial giants.

Here in America, the postwar expansion through the early 1970's was noteworthy for its conspicuous lack of major corrections, as well as for its longevity. There were several interim recessions. But they were all gentle and short-lived, stemming as they did mainly from temporary excesses in manufacturing and trade.

By way of contrast, the period between the two world wars witnessed two sharp business contractions, both of which were attributable to excesses in finance and both of which persisted for years. In fact, the Great Depression lasted a whole decade, despite all-out efforts by President Roosevelt to put business back on its feet.

Actually, the protracted depression of the 1930's and the Second World War were the very reasons why the economic expansion in the ensuing decades was so swift both at home and abroad. On the one hand, they created enormous demand for consumer and capital goods alike. On the other hand, they put the United States, its industrial plant unharmed by war and expanded during it, in a uniquely strong position to underwrite the subsequent world recovery.

How solid was the U.S. financial strength then? For openers, this country owned almost two-thirds of the world's monetary gold. Freely convertible into that precious metal, the dollar was literally as good as gold.

Even more important as regards domestic business, the entire private sector of the American economy was superliquid. During both the Depression and the War, private debt, relative to income and to financial assets, had trended persistently downward.

That ultra-liquid condition prevailing in the mid-1940's was well reflected in a wide range of banking statistics. For simplicity's sake, let's just look at the ratio of commercial bank loans to the amount of money on deposit with those banks.

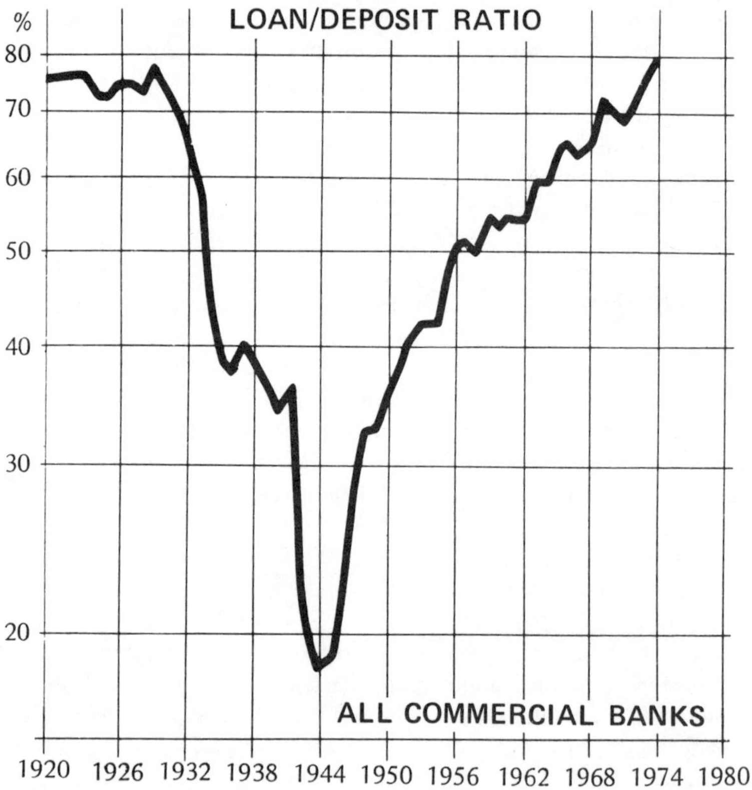

At the end of World War II, the loan-to-deposit ratio was unusually low. The banking system was exceptionally liquid. Since then, the ratio has risen to the highest level in more than half a century. Both banks and their customers have become quite illiquid.

At the end of World War II, that loan-to-deposit ratio was only roughly 20%. It means that of every dollar of deposit, commercial banks had loaned out only 20c. The balance was substantially invested in U.S. Treasury securities, which were readily marketable. In short, banks were bursting with lending power.

Bank loans—whether made to individuals or corporations—are generally short-term obligations of borrowers. Checking and time deposits, on the other hand, represent the liquid assets of bank customers. Thus, the ultra-low loan-to-deposit ratio also indicates that private individuals and corporations were exceptionally liquid as well. In other words, they had enormous borrowing power.

For those not familiar with the working of banking systems, let me just add that on a nationwide basis, new bank deposits are typically created when a customer deposits currency into his bank account, or when a commercial bank makes a loan by crediting the borrower's checking account. Against this background, the ultra-low loan-to-deposit ratio in 1945 further reveals that some 80% of the checking and savings account balances then outstanding represented depositors' free-and-clear financial assets, while only 20% was accounted for by bank borrowings.

To put that 20% figure in still better perspective, note that until it started to drop in late 1929, the loan-to-deposit ratio had stayed well above the 70% level consistently for at least three decades. Before the money panic of 1921, it had even topped 80% on many occasions. *The "super-liquidity" prevailing at the end of World War II was thus a very, very unusual phenomenon.*

I cannot overemphasize the importance of this. Only by recognizing this anomaly can one avoid regarding the expansion of the past thirty years as normal. And only then will one refrain from relying too heavily on the pattern of postwar recessions to anticipate future business contractions.

During the early 1940's, soaring war expenditures resulted in a marked increase in personal income. But some of it could not be spent on consumer goods, production of which was being cut back. After VJ Day, therefore, a spectacular postwar buying binge occurred. By 1950, just five years later, consumer expenditures for durable goods had more than tripled. That boom went a long way toward changing the attitudes bred by the pre-war Depression.

As a result, both businessmen and consumers gradually became less hesitant to borrow. They also found their bankers friendlier. Helped by ever-liberalizing amortization terms and ever-lowering down-payment needs, loan-financed purchases just rose and rose. And the economy grew and grew.

But debt climbed much faster. Between 1945 and 1974, the gross national product multiplied roughly 6½ times; but commercial bank loans, some 20 times! During those three decades, the loan-to-deposit ratio soared. By late 1974, it was standing just a shade below 80%—nearly four times higher than in 1945.

Whether the lofty level of late is dangerous or not is debatable. Because it's higher than in 1929, some observers now think that a wholesale credit collapse is unavoidable. Others experts argue, however, that the use of modern electronic aids should enable banks to maintain a higher loan-to-deposit ratio than in the horse-and-buggy days without endangering liquidity. I'll give my opinion on this later.

But two things are indisputable.The loan-to-deposit ratio simply cannot quadruple again in the next thirty years. It is impossible for banks to lend out more than 100% of deposits. Besides the need to prepare for unexpected increases in deposit withdrawals, these institutions must meet reserve requirements prescribed by the Federal Reserve Board.

Similarly, there's no way bank customers can continue increasing their borrowings at a rate many times faster than their income growth.

When one buys or flies now and pays later, he mortgages a portion of his future income. The more debt he incurs, the larger a portion of his future paycheck must be allocated to repaying debt. If something unforeseen causes his earnings to drop, a heavy debt burden would exert a severe squeeze on his budget. It could even put him into bankruptcy.

But even without any income interruption, there will sooner or later come a point when he will have committed as much of his future income as possible. Thereafter, his total interest expense

THE GREAT CREDIT EXPANSION

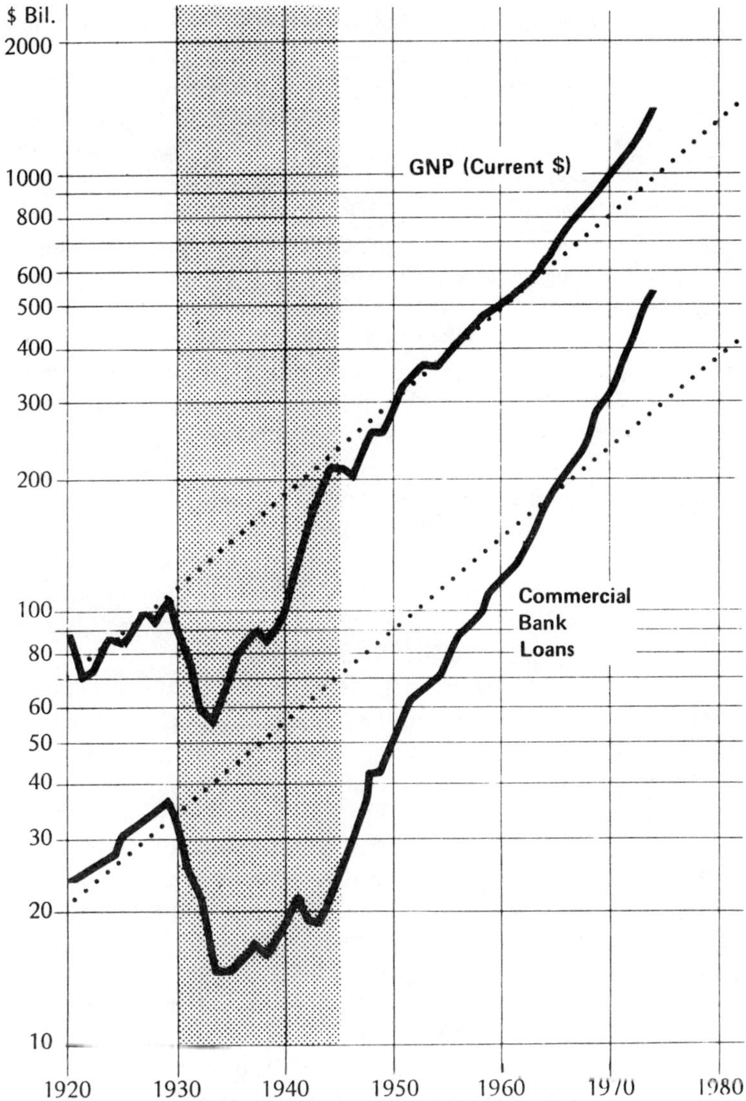

Economic growth in the past three decades has been financed by a rapid growth in commercial bank loans. The expansion prior to the mid-1960's made up for the drop in the early 1930's. The continued increase thereafter, however, has resulted in accelerated inflation.

and debt-repayment load can grow no faster than his take-home pay.

"Granted," you may say, "the growth in bank loans in the next thirty years will be slower than in the last thirty. But I just want to know what's going to happen in the next two or three years. Why should we assume that the loan-to-deposit ratio is peaking in 1974-75? Why not in 1978, 1980 or later?"

Good question. But many signs have emerged lately to suggest that for both banks and bank customers, the exhaustion point has indeed been reached.

For instance, in the last several years, the banking system has gone through quite a number of credit crunches. During this period, the Federal Reserve has actually pumped an unusually large amount of reserves into the banking system. Those repeated credit crunches, therefore, must be recognized as a distinct symptom of illiquidity. In short, relative to current deposits, the banking system has exhausted its lending power.

Signs of illiquidity among bank customers are also prevalent. In the past year or so, the number of personal bankruptcies, the liabilities of failed businesses, and the mortgage and installment-loan delinquency rates have all taken quantum leaps.

It is quite normal, of course, for a business slowdown to impair borrowers' ability to service or retire debt. And the economy did contract in 1974. But the jump in the last year or so has been far sharper than usual. Moreover, it had started climbing even before the economic decline set in. The implication: consumers as a whole already have as much debt as they reasonably can carry.

Moreover, it is an open secret that many banks and mortgage holders have been carrying billions of dollars of delinquent accounts without even collecting interest. They are obviously hoping that somehow those borrowers will eventually come through. Had they proceeded to collect or foreclose, both the delinquency and the bankruptcy rates would have been even higher.

There are also quite a number of positive developments revealing that the credit expansion cycle has peaked and that voluntary restraints are taking hold.

For the first time in decades, for instance, a number of leading commercial banks—including the Bank of America, the nation's largest—publicly stated recently that they had begun pursuing a more conservative loan policy. They are now placing more emphasis on increasing the quality of loan portfolios and less on boosting the volume of loan business.

On the other side of the loan desk, many bank customers have also been trimming down their obligations. At least from late 1974 through early 1975, repayment of consumer installment debt far exceeded new extensions—a distinct reversal of the postwar trend. In the first half of 1975, likewise, commercial and industrial bank loans trended significantly downward—also a clear departure from previous experience.

In light of all these developments, the nearly 80% loan-to-deposit ratio must be acknowledged as being awfully close to the practical ceiling. A further rise from this point, if it should occur, will be due not so much to an acceleration of loan extensions as to a decline in loan retirements. Such a rise would create more dislocation and add little to real economic expansion. We can therefore safely assume that business growth in the second half of the 1970's will, at the very best, be much slower than in the past.

Now, let's see how the past three decades of rapid debt growth has affected the supply-and-demand situation. For one thing, borrowing more and more money to pay for current consumption has undoubtedly enabled both individuals and businesses to buy much more in the past than they could normally afford. For that reason, business activities in recent years must have run at a much higher level than what the economy could really support. It also means that once purchases of goods and services are no longer supplemented by debt-financed buying, they will drop to a level more consistent with what the buyers can truly afford.

The rapid increase in bank loans, along with mounting fiscal deficits by the government, has also contributed to inflation. When new buying power is artificially created by banks via a bookkeeping entry, there is no offsetting increase in the supply of goods or services. Prices have got to go up to compensate for the difference.

Note in this connection that in 1972 and 1973 alone, commercial bank loans jumped some $144 billion, nearly triple the increase in the preceding two years. Because of the time-delay factor, inflation reached the two-digit level in 1974.

Because inflation cuts the real spendable income of the consumer, what he can afford to buy has been declining. As a result, real consumer demand, especially for goods that are usually bought on credit, cannot help but remain at a reduced level for some time.

Nevertheless, business and industry have already geared up their capacity to meet the inflated demand of the early 1970's. Some companies, in fact, are still making long-term plans on the assumption that the economy will continue to grow at the abnormal rate of the past. The result must be that capacity, already excessive, will become even more so when expansion projects now under construction are completed. The resultant cutbacks in capital investment will further dampen business activity in the years ahead.

Slower real economic growth also means smaller increases in personal income. But many borrowers had counted on a continuation of the rapid rise in purchasing power. The developing slowdown in real economic growth thus represents the "something unforeseen" I mentioned earlier that will squeeze many a family's budget. After applying an unexpectedly larger portion of current income to service and retire outstanding debt, the consumer will have relatively less to spend.

Thus, in contrast to the last thirty years, when the demand generated by earned income was supplemented by debt-created buying power, purchases of goods and services in the remaining half of this decade will actually fall below the demand corresponding to current income. Therefore, the real national output in the late 1970's probably won't be significantly higher than that of the early 1970's.

All this also implies that over the coming years, bank loans will grow more slowly than the economy. During a period of business contraction, they may even contract. Since the need to expand manufacturing facilities will be nearly nonexistent for a while, corporate long-term debt will probably follow the same pattern. Thus, total supply of goods and services will rise faster, or fall slower, than demand. And a trend of lowering prices will emerge.

True, quotations of individual items may go up here and there; but for the economy as a whole, deflation will gradually replace inflation.

A gradual reduction in the debt ratio will make the economy leaner, thereby paving the way for healthy expansion in the 1980's. Replacing inflation with deflation will also be beneficial to consumers, especially those living on fixed or nearly fixed incomes. Liberal politicians will, no doubt, consider any slowdown in the rate of economic growth socially unacceptable. But they will not be able to change free-market forces much.

State and local governments certainly cannot help prime the economic pump. Municipal taxes have already risen so much that in recent years more and more Americans have been registering their displeasure at the voting booth. As income growth becomes harder to come by, the tax revolt will intensify. Governors and mayors alike will find it necessary to actually cut expenditures, especially when tax revenues are shaved by a business slowdown.

Although federal tax revenues will also experience slower growth, Washington will be in a better position to increase spending. It will have fewer problems selling securities to finance budget deficits. But in recent years, federal purchases of goods and services have accounted for less than 8.5% of the gross national product. Put another way, the rest of the economy is more than ten times larger. For that reason, at least in the years immediately ahead, federal spending can hardly increase enough, barring a new world war, to fully offset the slowdown in the giant private sector.

By the same token, the prospective increase in federal debt, while staggering by past standards, will not prevent a significant slowdown in the growth of *total* debt from occurring. At the end of 1974, federal debt, including securities issued by government agencies, amounted to $437 billion. But individuals, corporations and state and local governments combined owed as much as $2.34 *trillion*. This is why I foresee softening prices in the years ahead instead of the runaway inflation that many pessimists now predict.

Although the national unemployment rate will probably rise

well above the 10% level in the late 1970's, I also do not believe widespread social disorder will result. There are far more two-earner families nowadays than in the 1950's. Moreover, tiding the unemployed over and creating work for able-bodied youngsters are what the federal government can and, I believe, will do effectively. On the plus side, a sustained period of high unemployment will probably induce union leaders to scale down on their wage demands.

What about those dire predictions of wholesale bank failures? I think they, too, are too pessimistic. True, banks will be hurt by substantial uncollectible loans, and a few institutions will become insolvent. But even if it had to "print" money, the Federal Reserve Board can and will keep major banks intact.

Most importantly, both banks and bank customers, as I explained, have voluntarily been shoring up their liquidity position. Conditions in the summer of 1975 were already much healthier than they were in mid-1974. This is precisely how free-market forces correct imbalances. To expect the highly unusual 1929-33 collapse to be repeated is about as unrealistic as to consider the mild postwar recessions normal.

Summing up, based on evidence now available, I believe the economy during the remaining years of this decade will be sluggish compared with that of the past thirty years. Total output in the late 1970's will not be significantly higher, if higher at all, than in the early 1970's. Manufacturing capacity will be excessive. Because total demand will fall below total supply, prices in general will soften. The unemployment rate will remain high, but no social revolution is in prospect. Personal and corporate bankruptcies will rise, but there will be no collapse of the banking system. The fiscal deficit will soar, but the growth in total debt will slow. Reversing their 30-year uptrend, interest rates in general will move downward. All in all, the second half of the Sobering Seventies will be quite different from the first half.

CHAPTER 16

Wait Till They Cry "Uncle!"

THE ECONOMY ABROAD will be quite different also. To help envision the future, let us again review the past.

The Second World War left most countries in Western Europe and Japan all but devastated. For the most part, their industries were crippled, their central banks broke. By way of contrast, the War helped the U. S. to emerge from its decade-long Depression. Spared from enemy bombs and missiles, American factories were able to produce at full throttle to supply allied countries.

Partly to prevent a Communist takeover of the then highly vulnerable world, the U.S. immediately launched major foreign aid programs to help rebuild former enemies as well as allies. But those tens of billions of dollars poured abroad were also meant to keep the American economy from relapsing into its pre-war Depression. Much of that money had to be spent buying U.S. goods.

Some of the foreign aid money, nevertheless, had to be spent locally. Also, many U.S. corporations joined the reconstruction program by investing in foreign countries. As a result, there was a substantial outflow of U.S. dollars, which eventually reached the coffers of foreign central banks. That development was welcomed by most countries. They needed foreign capital badly.

Moreover, even before the War ended, plans had been mapped out at Bretton Woods, New Hampshire, for a new international monetary system. Under that agreement, both the British pound sterling and the U.S. dollar were recognized as reserve currencies, an asset that could be used in lieu of gold. The system also called for fixed exchange rates among major currencies and for the U.S. to readily buy and sell gold at the then official $35-an-ounce rate. Since America had an enormous gold stock but small liquid liabilities to foreigners, the dollar was, in fact, an unquestioned proxy for the metal. As such, the increasing amounts of greenbacks held by foreign central bankers helped to bolster those countries' reserve assets.

As the world recovery proceeded, one developed country after another became our competitor. With plants newly built, many of their industries were modern and efficient. Their labor forces were not usually as skilled as those in America, but that was more than offset by substantially lower wages. It's not surprising, therefore, that foreign-made goods were soon outselling American products, at least in those areas where foreign-aid restrictions did not apply.

This fact, along with attractive tax incentives offered by many foreign governments, further encouraged American corporations to invest and build plants abroad. Result: made-in-America goods encountered still tougher competition. Had it not been for exports dictated by foreign-aid programs, the U.S. balance of trade would long ago have shown sizable deficits. But because of them, there were consistent trade surpluses. Many Americans became complacent as a result. Consequently, more and more dollars went abroad. The U.S. balance of payments fell deeper and deeper into the red.

Bulging with dollars, some foreign central bankers systematically exchanged part of their excess holdings for U.S. gold in the 1950's. Reflecting the continuing payments deficit on the one hand and the sale of U.S. gold to foreign central banks on the other, total U.S. liquid liabilities to foreigners finally exceeded the U.S. gold holdings in the late 1950's.

THE REAL INTERNATIONAL MONEY PROBLEM

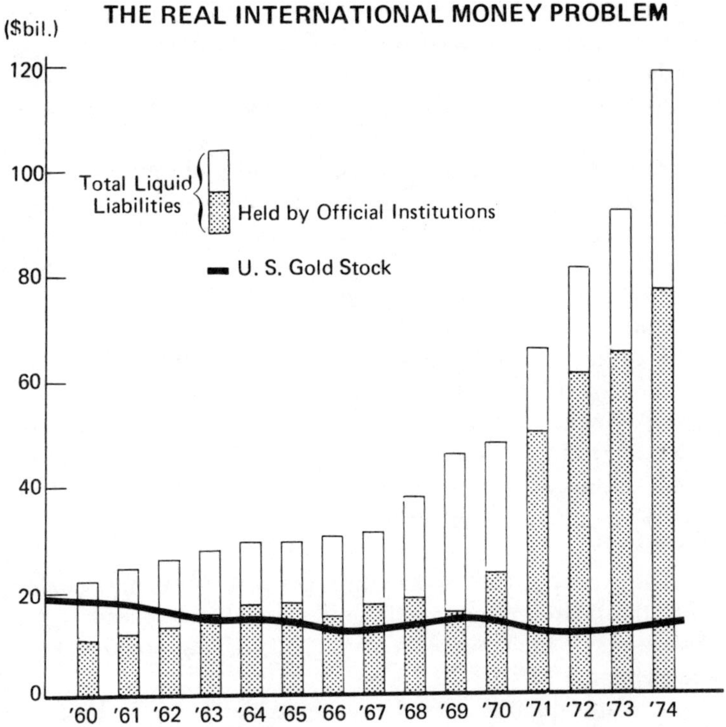

Total U.S. Liquid Liabilities to foreigners have been rising persistently. U.S. Gold Stock, on the other hand, has trended generally downward. That's why the U.S. cannot afford to let the dollar be convertible into gold.

The eventual realization of that fact by the public prompted many individuals to buy gold on the open market. In 1960, the private demand was so strong that the open market price in Europe jumped to $41 an ounce. To push the free-market price back down to the official rate, leading industrial countries formed a gold pool to sell official holdings to the public. The U.S. Treasury was by far the biggest supplier.

Formation of the pool did cool the gold fever for a while. But neither the U.S. Treasury nor foreign central bankers took advantage of the time gained to nip the developing world money problem in the bud. No one seriously worried about the fact that foreign dollar holdings were no longer fully backed by gold.

In the early 1960's, fewer countries received U.S. aid than in the late 1940's and the 1950's. But those who did still had to apply much of the windfall to buy U.S. goods. Thus, the American balance of trade continued to show healthy surpluses. But because the capital outflow resulting from foreign-aid payments and from capital investments abroad was heavier, the balance of payments remained consistently in the red. Thus, foreign holdings of U.S. dollars kept increasing and the U.S. gold stock kept shrinking.

Still, government officials were complacent. The U.S. was perfectly happy with the situation. It only had to pay a small portion of the payments deficit bill. Meanwhile, the foreign-aid money was a boon to U. S. exporters. And major corporations were able to keep increasing their investments abroad without worrying about the resultant dollar outflow.

Foreign countries, too, were perfectly satisfied with the situation. The inflow of U.S. money brought with it booming business across the board. Foreign economies could not otherwise have grown as fast; their people's standard of living could not have risen as high.

By the mid-1960's, total U.S. liquid liabilities to foreigners were almost twice as large as the U.S. gold stock. The dollars held by foreign official institutions alone exceeded the U.S. gold holdings. Now a few central bankers began to worry. But to avoid upsetting the applecart, monetary leaders agreed to pooh-pooh the situation.

The fact that a substantial amount of those officially held dollars were then in Japan and Germany also helped the Treasury somewhat. Those two countries depended heavily on American armed forces for their national defense. Washington was thus able to pressure them to refrain from buying U. S. gold.

Meanwhile, Britain was also living beyond its means while the pound sterling was also being held by central banks as a reserve asset. For years, Britain had sustained substantial payment deficits as well. But Britain's international trade position was not propped up by foreign-aid money. It kept weakening. In an attempt to remedy the situation, that country surprised the world by devaluing the pound in November 1967. Though central bankers put on a calm front, worldwide confidence in both reserve currencies was immediately and seriously shaken.

In early 1968, the public's mistrust was translated into a gold-buying binge. Major central banks in general and the U.S. in particular were losing gold so rapidly through the London gold pool that they decided to stop the sale of official holdings to the public by abandoning the pool. The so-called two-tier market—one for free-market gold and one for official gold—was then born.

But eliminating private foreigners' claims on U.S. gold was not enough. The dollars held by official institutions at that time were still well above the U. S. gold stock. To keep the monetary world calm, Washington kept pressuring foreign central banks not to exchange dollars for gold. In return, it promised these creditors that the U.S. would soon end its recurring payments deficits.

But to eliminate the payments deficits, the U.S. would have to slow down the domestic economy, something politically unattractive. So the Treasury came up with a new argument. If dollars return to the U.S., it contended, the world would suffer from an insufficiency of reserve assets and international trade would be seriously hurt. It was not really a valid argument, but so many monetary planners believed it that they responded by inducing the International Monetary Fund to create a new super-money—Special Drawing Rights (SDR's)—to replace the dollar as the secondary reserve asset.

In the early 1970's, billions of dollars worth of SDR's were created. But the U.S. payments deficits continued. Now the world had too much reserve assets. Inflation, which had hitherto been creeping in most major countries, accelerated.

Meanwhile, worried Americans more and more began to buy foreign currencies that had stronger gold backing. As a result, those currencies rose in value in the foreign-exchange market and the dollar dropped. But under terms of the monetary agreement worked out back in 1944, central bankers had to maintain the established exchange rate within a narrow range. To keep the dollar from falling below the limit, they had to buy greenbacks on the open market, issuing their own currencies in the process. As a result, dollar holdings of foreign central banks swelled, and their own money supplies expanded sharply. This expansion added oil to the inflation fire in their countries.

By 1971, dollar holdings by official foreign institutions were equivalent to roughly three times the U.S. gold stock. In the summer, a few countries ignored the Treasury's pleas and bought some gold from the U.S. As other countries were lining up to follow suit, President Nixon had to close the gold window, thereby making the dollar unconvertible.

Detaching the dollar from gold also put an end to fixed currency-exchange rates. Since the exchange value of most currencies had been expressed in units of gold via the dollar, the divorce of the dollar from gold unfixed all exchange rates. The era of floating exchange rates thus began.

To many, the idea of floating exchange rates sounded good at first. If demand for currency A is much greater than demand for currency B, why not let A go up in value and let B go down? That's the free-market system, isn't it?

But floating currency rates make just about as much sense as floating the conversion table between the metric and the conventional measuring system.

As we all know, a yard equals 36 inches. A meter is somewhat longer; it is equivalent to 39.37 inches. But can you imagine someone saying: "More and more countries are now using the metric system, so the demand for the meter-stick is getting greater than that for the yardstick. To adjust for this free-market change in demand, let's make the meter shorter and the yard longer. Better yet, why not let the relationship between the two float during business hours?"

Fortunately, engineers have enough common sense to know that both the meter and the yard are *standards of measure;* they have nothing to do with market forces. The same should hold true with national currencies. One of the three functions of money is to be a *standard of value.* (To be a store of value and a means of exchange are the other two.) As standards of value, currencies are not commodities. To let their exchange rates float is to destroy their usefulness as money.

As was to be expected, floating rates have been disruptive to international trade. Excessive swings have already brought down a few banks. And to prevent exchange rate changes from eroding their profits, merchants doing international business have found it necessary to tie up considerable working capital engaging in the currency hedging operations.

But not all businesses can afford that. As a result, international trade, after having been temporarily buoyed by widespread commodity speculation in 1973-74, has since slowed. By mid-1975, there were distinct signs that the 30-year upward trend had been reversed. Despite inflated prices, total world exports dropped far below the year-earlier level.

After the gold window was closed, confidence in the dollar eroded still more. An additional $50 billion or so has moved out of the U.S. That outflow immediately increased the money supplies in major foreign countries, sharply accelerating their inflation rates. It was ironic that U.S. Government spokesmen took comfort during the early 1970's in the fact that inflation was worse abroad than at home. The U.S. was primarily responsible for that distortion.

By late 1974, foreign countries had learned something new: the United States was able to export depression as well as inflation. Since dollars held abroad cannot now be presented to the Treasury to be exchanged for gold, the U.S. no longer had to worry about sustaining even monstrous payments deficits. For that reason, this country could purposely let its currency sink in the foreign exchange market, especially since the U.S. does not depend heavily on imports.

A devalued dollar enables American exporters to enjoy a stronger competitive position. They can price their goods cheaper in the world market. This fact became clear in late 1974 and in early 1975. The dollar underwent a major sinking spell, and the export business of countries abroad suffered immediately thereafter. As a result, foreign leaders have since wanted to return to a fixed exchange system and to stop the dollar outflow.

From Washington's standpoint, any return to fixed exchange rates would proscribe the U.S. from artificially depressing the dollar to help domestic industries, and any system disallowing indefinite payments deficits would require the U.S. to implement unpopular austerity measures. Both are politically unacceptable.

Moreover, restoring gold as a reserve unit could cost the U.S. its entire gold stock. The fact is, even with gold valued at a price of, say, $200 an ounce, the Treasury's gold holdings would only be worth about $55 billion. In mid-1975, total U.S. liquid liabilities to foreigners amounted to over $110 billion, of which roughly $80 billion were accounted for by official institutions. *The reason the U.S. wants to phase gold out of the world monetary system is to preserve its gold holdings.*

In a nutshell, then, the best interests of the United States and those of most industrialized foreign countries are diametrically opposed and irreconcilable. In the coming years, some stopgap agreements may be reached, but no meaningful international monetary reform can be expected. The impasse will keep decelerating world trade, resulting in a widespread economic slowdown abroad.

To combat the contraction, most countries will probably resort to boosting government spending and/or nationalizing banks and industries. They will literally print money to keep the economy going. Unlike in the U.S., the inflationary pressure so generated will not be offset by deflationary forces in the private sectors. As a result, inflation will continue abroad even while deflation unfolds here. In the foreign exchange market, the dollar will strengthen while most other currencies will weaken. Before long, the U.S. will be wanting a return to fixed exchange rates, but foreign countries will oppose this.

Meanwhile, the recent sharp rise in the oil price has also served to retard business activity worldwide. Tens of billions of dollars of spending money are being taken out of consuming countries and only a part of those revenues are being respent by the oil-producing nations. For the world as a whole, there has thus been an increase in saving, and a drop in spending. As long as this situation continues, the total demand for all goods and services, including petroleum products, will keep softening. Let me stress, though, that even if oil prices had not soared, business activities throughout the world would still have been shrinking. Free-market forces will correct for man-made excesses one way or another.

The prospective recovery of the dollar in the foreign-exchange market will feed on itself. As more and more dollars return from abroad, there will be a significant improvement in the U.S. balance of payments. That in turn will further strengthen the dollar and weaken foreign currencies and will stimulate additional dollar inflow. In the 1980's, foreign dollar holdings will probably have been cut by many tens of billions.

The return flow of the dollar will further weaken the economy abroad since many of those dollars had helped stimulate demand. In short, the remainder of this decade will witness a sluggish economy all over the world.

Chances are, therefore, that some years from now, most governments will finally be totally frustrated with the protracted economic contraction. Only then will monetary leaders have a common interest in restoring order to the international monetary system so that world trade can resume growing. Only then will they be willing to subordinate domestic political considerations to the need for international cooperation. Only then will they be able to make solid progress toward a realistic monetary reform.

The next workable world monetary system, I believe, will restore fixed exchange rates among currencies. It will be based on a monetary unit that is both a store and a standard of value. This primary reserve unit, of course, will not be anything easily printed on paper or created by accounting entries. It will be something of lasting value.

Since gold has proven its worth as being something durable and portable and has been recognized worldwide over thousands of years as something of value, it will probably be used again as such a standard. Based on the probable money supplies outstanding in industrialized countries around 1980, I estimate that the next official price will be around $200 an ounce, give or take $25.

With U.S. liquid liabilities to foreigners substantially reduced, the dollar will then become convertible and will again be as good as gold.

CHAPTER 17

One Up, One Down

WITH THE FLOW-OF-FUNDS approach, let us now try to see how these domestic and international economic prospects are likely to be reflected in the stock and bond markets. With a little logic, let us examine how they will affect the various buying and selling groups. Again, we will limit our study here to analyzing the long-term trend only.

As I explained back in Chapter 11, the key factors controlling the supply and demand relationship can be divided into four primary classifications: Private Individuals, Institutional Investors, Corporations, and Others. I normally subdivide them into more than 20 smaller groups to facilitate the study of the market's short- and intermediate-term movements. But to avoid getting bogged down in minute details, I shall just illustrate how I put the Flow-of-Funds approach to work by analyzing the major classifications. And, instead of making absolute projections, I shall show you how to anticipate probable trend changes.

Let's take the bond market first. We have already established that interest rates in general, after having risen for three decades, will probably trend downward in the years ahead. Since the price of outstanding bonds moves in the opposite direction from interest rates, the bond market is thus expected to firm.

This prospect is well supported by the Flow-of-Funds study. The chart on this page shows the net purchases or sales of corporate and foreign bonds by private households in the last 20 years. (All charts here are based on FRB data.)

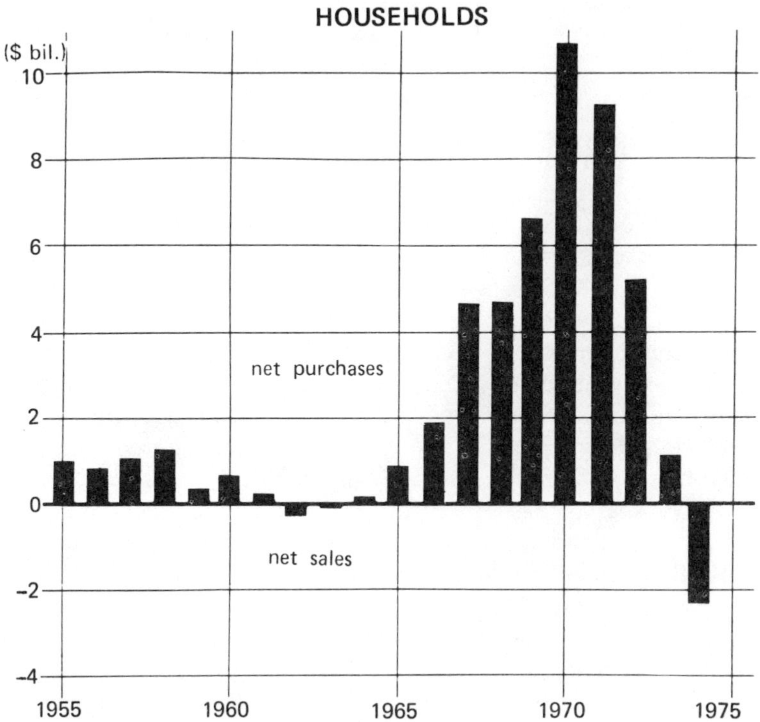

Note that the general public, which had stayed pretty much away from the bond market prior to 1966, became enthusiastic buyers around the turn of the decade. In 1973 and 1974, however, they lost interest in corporate bonds again.

The public's apathy in the decade prior to 1966 is quite understandable. Bond yields were very low then—lower, in fact, than what savings banks were paying. The public's subsequent love affair with fixed-income issues is easily explained. In 1970, high-grade corporates were yielding close to 8% on the average, compared to less than 4½% in 1965 and only about 3% back in 1955.

But what happened in 1973 and 1974? Corporate bonds continued to offer near-record yields, yet households became net sellers of these securities.

The answer is that private investors found something else that provided equally lush income but even greater safety. They invested over $35 billion in U.S. Government securities during that same period. In the preceding two years, there had been net *liquidation* of such issues of nearly $14 billion. What happened was that the yields from Treasury bills soared in 1973 and 1974. The average return available from 90-day bills, for example, topped 8% on many occasions. The public switched its allegiance in response. All this only confirms that most private investors are keenly income-conscious.

What about the years ahead? Treasury bill yields have already dropped considerably since mid-1974. There will be some interim rises. But in the scenario I foresee, they will probably remain well below corporate bond yields. To be sure, as bond prices rise in a sluggish economy, bond yields will also dip. But they will remain considerably more generous than the income offered by most blue-chip common stocks and savings banks.

Accordingly, we can safely assume that net purchases of bonds by private individuals will be running at a rate much closer to that prevailing around the turn of the decade than in either 1973-74 or the decade before 1966.

What will financial institutional investors do? The record for the last 20 years is illustrated by the accompanying chart.

Old-line institutions like insurance companies have typically been major buyers of corporate bonds, if only because they are required to do so by law to be conservative. But note that throughout the 1960's, net purchases by institutional investors as a whole held rather steady. It was only in the last three years that they started accumulating these securities heavily. Net buying in 1974 was particularly pronounced, exceeding the year-earlier total by some 80%.

There is every reason to expect this group to remain big bond-

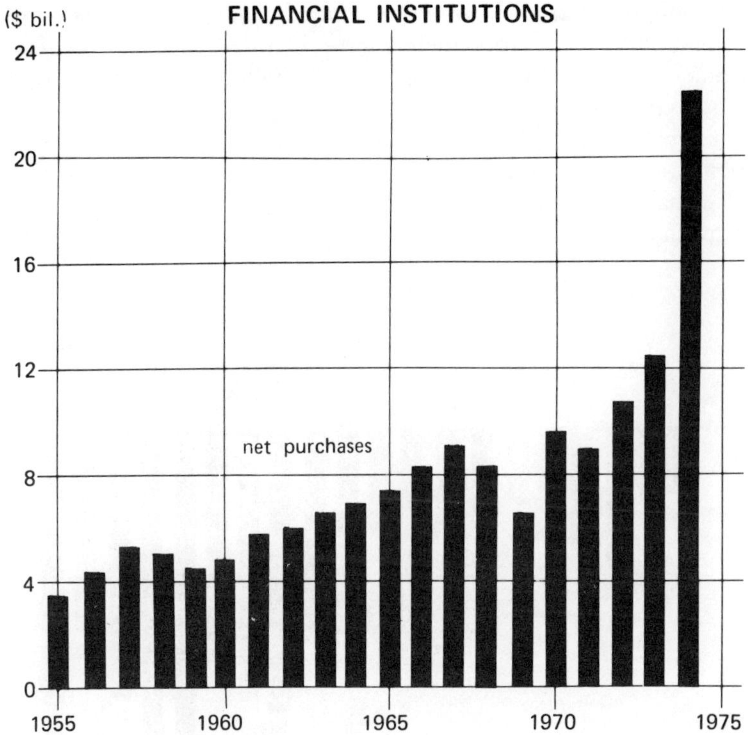

buyers in the coming years. More and more trustees and portfolio supervisors of pension and retirement funds have learned the hard way that playing the stock market can be terribly costly, and that investing in fixed-income securities involves much less risk. The fact that yields from corporate bonds are generally well above actuarial requirements also helps.

Moreover, the Pension Reform Act of 1974 has made many involved with these funds more aware of their awesome fiduciary responsibilities and of the need to invest prudently. Certainly, buying high-grade bonds is one way to practice prudent investing.

For both stocks and bonds, the changes in net sales or purchases by "Other" investors, including foreigners, are generally not significant enough to make any serious impact on the long-term trend. But in the emerging era wherein the dollar is expected to strengthen relative to other currencies, many foreigners will probably want to store their capital in the U.S. for a change. Some of this inflow of foreign money will undoubtedly find its way to the bond market.

Corporations, of course, are almost always net sellers of bonds. As such, they regularly withdraw funds from this market. The chart on this page shows the net outflow resulting from bond sales in the past 20 years.

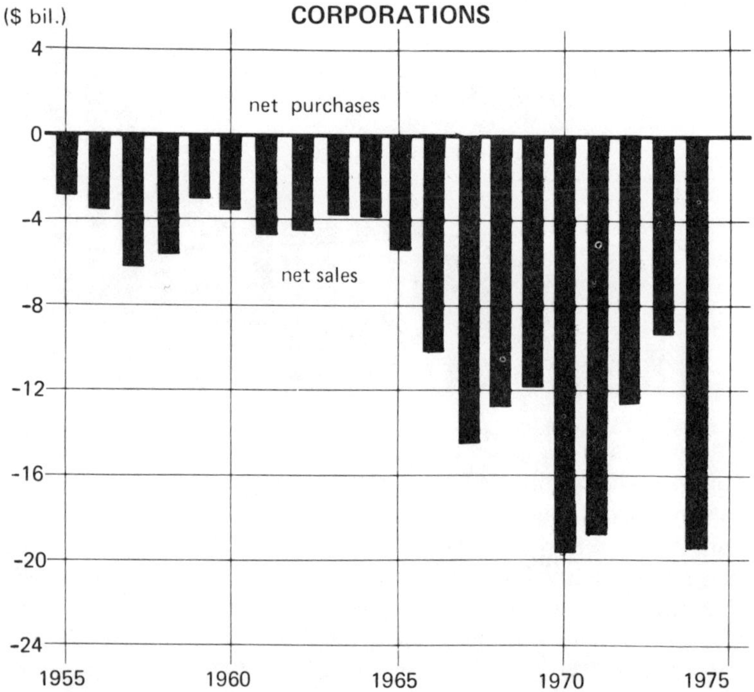

Corporations typically seek more and more outside capital as business expands. The upward trend in bond offerings over the past two decades thus is normal.

The drop in 1972-73 from the much higher 1970-71 total, however, was unusual. What happened? Bond yields, after having peaked in the middle of 1970, declined somewhat in 1971. In 1972 and 1973, corporate treasurers anticipated a further drop in long-term rates. So, many withheld new offerings and "temporarily" borrowed from commercial banks to satisfy their cash requirements.

But they outsmarted themselves. Bond yields climbed sharply again in 1974. But these corporations could no longer continue to borrow short to finance long-term needs. They rushed back to sell bonds heavily in 1974 (and even more so in the first half of 1975).

The scenario I foresee for the remainder of this decade involves a significant slowing in business activities. Most industries will have more than ample capacity and little need to expand. Capital outlays can be substantially financed with internal cash flow. For that reason, new bond offerings will probably run at a much lower rate than in 1974-75.

All told, therefore, the Flow-of-Funds study indicates that, compared with recent years, corporations will be taking less money out from the bond market in the second half of the 1970's, and that private individuals, institutional investors and foreigners will all put more funds into this market. This means rising bond prices.

I recognize, of course, that in the years ahead the federal government will seek an enormous amount of capital to help finance its fiscal deficits. The bulk of the financing, however, will probably be made through the sale of Treasury securities maturing in five years or less. They will not compete directly with long-term corporate issues.

Furthermore, the Fed is almost certain to keep pumping reserves into the banking system. But with loan demand softening in my economic scenario, most banks will find it necessary to put their excess reserves to work by buying Treasury issues. Thanks to the fractional reserve system, with every dollar of new reserves, the banking system can buy many, many dollars of Treasury securities.

Finally, more and more of those excess dollars that the Organization of Petroleum Exporting Countries have been accumulating will find their way into the U.S. Treasury market. During the 18 months ending in mid-1975, such purchases totalled an estimated $15 billion. With fewer safe investments available elsewhere in a slowing economy and with the dollar strengthening in the world market, the OPEC group will undoubtedly find these issues even more attractive.

What about the stock market? Let's follow the same procedure to find out what the major groups are likely to do.

In the past two decades, households have been net sellers almost three-quarters of the time. Their net purchases and net sales are shown on the chart below.

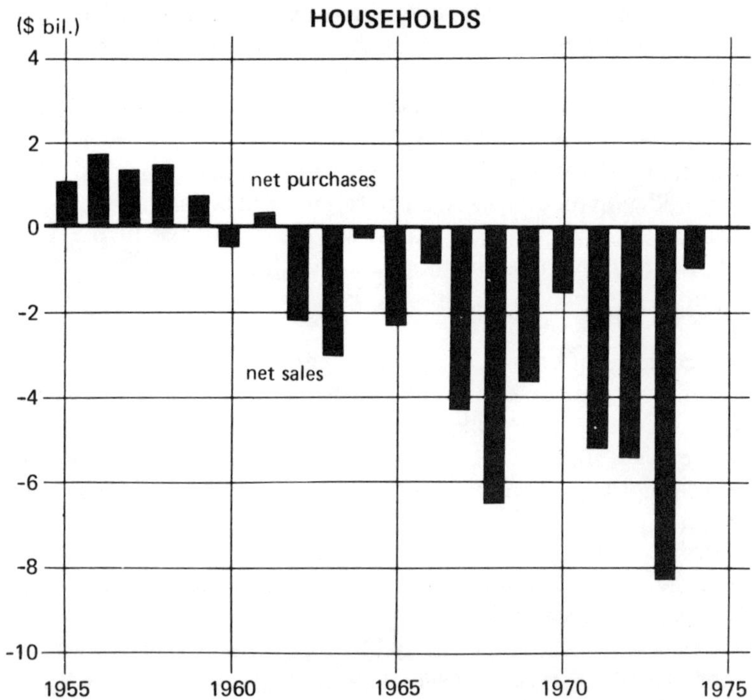

The pattern is significant in at least three respects:

1) Even though the number of investors kept increasing through the early 1970's, private households as a group have been net sellers of corporate equities for about 15 years. The sellers must therefore have been veteran investors of considerable

means, each liquidating much more stock than the purchases of many new investors combined.

For the group as a whole, net liquidation began in the early 1960's, when stock yields fell clearly below those offered by bonds and savings banks. This preference for safe and high yields, I believe, will induce these substantial investors to keep taking funds out of the stock market. Compared to bonds, most blue-chip stocks still offer rather low yields. And many secondary companies are likely to cut dividends in the slow economy ahead.

2) Since the number of investors did increase between the early 1960's and a few years ago, many millions of new shareholders of lesser means entered the stock market for the first time during that period. Most of these latecomers are presumably growth-oriented. Thus, the first two legs of the primary bear market—the 1969-70 and the 1973-74 declines—have already brought them bitter disappointment. As the business contraction I foresee unfolds, more and more such investors will want to get out of the equity market altogether.

3) As a group, private investors are also price-conscious. For example, they were net buyers in the 1950's, when stocks were cheap. They then became net sellers after stocks had climbed to much higher levels. In the past decade, they reduced their net liquidation markedly in 1966 and 1970 and in 1974—the very three years when the market registered its three major bottoms.

In the summer of 1975, the investing public was selling heavily again—although stock prices had recovered only about half the losses sustained in the 1973-74 plunge. In short, they had evidently lowered the level at which they considered stocks too high.

Given the slow economy in prospect, chances are these investors will instinctively consider more and more stocks dearly priced in the years ahead and will therefore continue to unload. The market may thus have to sink well below the 1974 bottom before these investors reduce their liquidation significantly again.

Financial institutions have in effect been supporting the stock market singlehandedly in recent years. The chart shows how much money they have pumped into equities over the past two decades.

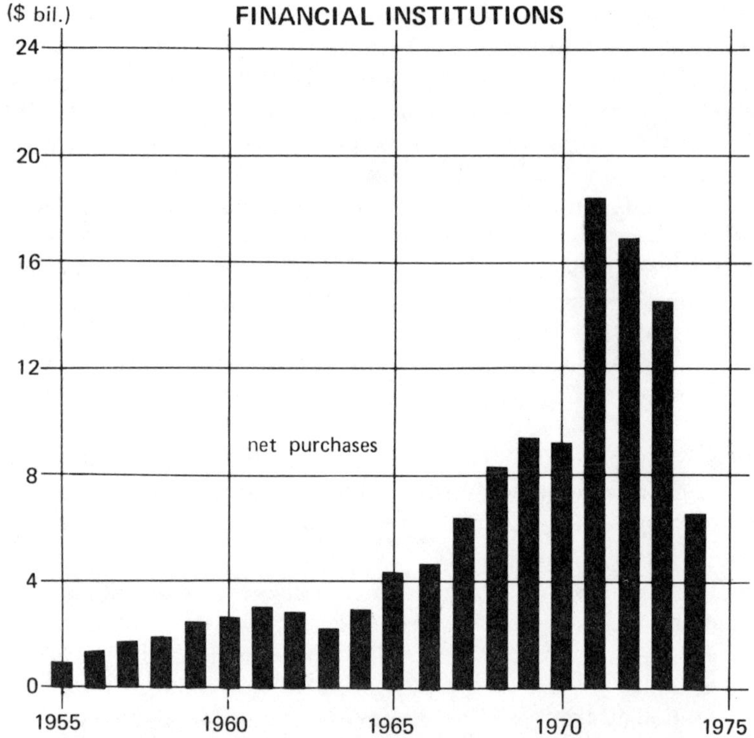

Unlike private individuals, these institutions have the distinguished record of having bought stocks timidly when prices were low and boldly when prices were high. In 1971 through 1973, when the Dow Jones industrials average was surging to and then retreating from its all-time peak, these institutions injected nearly six times as much new money in equities as they did ten years earlier, when stocks were much cheaper.

Note, however, that while institutions bought heavily in 1970, when the market made its first bear-market low, they did trim their net purchases measurably in 1974, when the market made its second bear-market low. This fact, together with the heavy institutional purchases of bonds discussed earlier, indicates that many funds have indeed decided to play it safe by investing in senior securities. If so, net purchases of common stocks by at least the old-line institutions will probable stay relatively low from this point forward.

To be sure, some of the pension funds managed by the big banks did resume buying the glamour issues heavily in the first half of 1975. But the money managers who supervise these portfolios are distinctly economy-oriented. As the economy softens under my economic scenario, these experts will be among the first to turn bearish. Toward the end of this decade, they may even be net sellers of common stocks.

Just as they are net sellers in the bond market, corporations are usually net sellers of stocks. Whenever they issue new shares for cash, funds are removed from the stock market. However, on those rare occasions when new offerings are limited and when corporations reacquire a substantial amount of their own shares, a net inflow of funds into the market does result. The chart shows their flow pattern for the past twenty years.

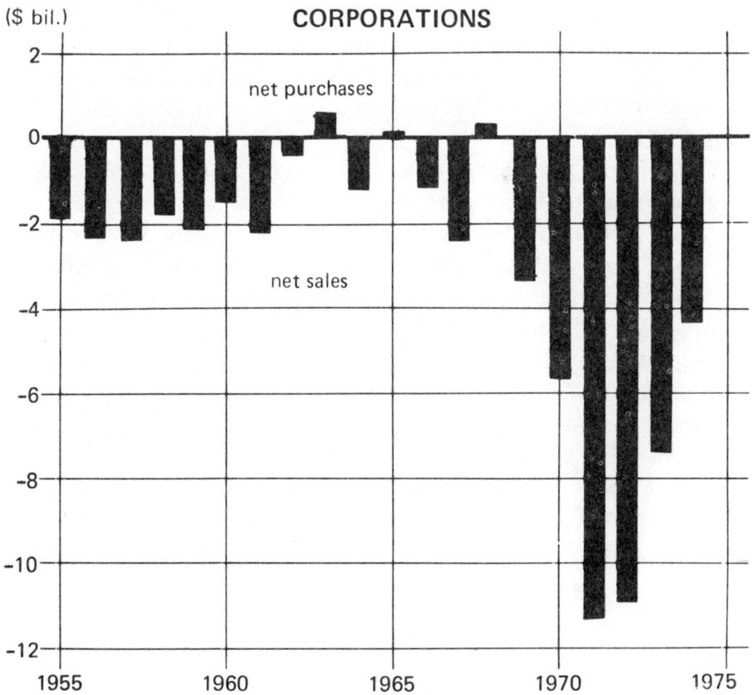

Like the issuance of new bonds, net equity offerings have generally trended upward over the past two decades. Note, however, that in 1973 and 1974, the funds they raised in the stock market totalled only $11.5 billion. That compares with over $22 billion in the preceding two years. The reason, of course, is that new equities were hard to sell during the bear market.

But it was during that very same superboom that corporations were desperately in need of outside capital. Besides mounting capital expenditures, they had to carry increasing accounts receivable and ever-costlier inventories. As I pointed out earlier, many firms resorted to bank borrowings as well as bond offerings.

In the economic scenario for the remainder of this decade, overall corporate needs for external funds will subside considerably. Nevertheless, stock offerings during these years may actually run higher than the depressed level of 1973-74. Many firms, especially utilities, must augment their equity capital.

After some 30 years of uninterrupted debt expansion, the equity-to-debt ratio of industry as a whole has been dropping persistently. This is acceptable in good times. But large fixed interest expenses will represent an awesome burden in a protracted economic slowdown.

Worse yet, a good portion of most corporations' current assets is represented by accounts receivable. In the sluggish economy ahead, any number of companies will find more and more receivables uncollectible. As corporate equities are adjusted downward to reflect the writeoff of these illusory assets, the equity-to-debt ratio will drop further. To stay solvent, quite a few corporations will have to sell new shares, even at depressed prices.

Summing up, in the years ahead I believe the money to be taken out of the stock market by private investors will remain heavy—certainly higher than in 1974. The amount of funds absorbed by corporations will probably run at about the same rate as in 1973-74. On the other hand, new capital injected into the equity market by institutional investors will trend clearly downward. On balance, therefore, the market will remain under substantial selling pressure.

This suggests that the primary bear market that started at the end of 1968 has at least one more major leg to go. This time around, institutional favorites that make up the market's recent upper tier are likely to suffer the largest drop, for three reasons: 1) low-yield stocks are least attractive to the investing public; 2) corporations with overpriced stocks are the ones most willing to issue new shares; and 3) financial institutions will put fewer dollars to support these issues.

Before I close this chapter, let me emphasize once again that the overview of the Flow-of-Funds analysis above pertains only to the long-term stock market trend. Even if no significant revisions are required in the future, there will be interim advances that offer handsome profit opportunities. Anticipating a downward trend for the market does not preclude in any way taking advantage of bear-market advances when they do occur.

CHAPTER 18

Beating the Experts the Easy Way

NOW, YOU KNOW WHY I anticipate stocks to trend downward and bonds to trend upward in the second half of this decade. More importantly, you also know what key assumptions I used and how I arrived at these conclusions. Note that my whole analytical process was based on 1) an objective study of world economic and monetary developments, 2) common-sense interpretation of past flows of funds into and out of the market, and 3) reasonable assumptions of how prospective developments will affect these flows in the future. Nowhere did my personal preferences enter the picture.

If you agree with my assumptions, fine. But even if you don't, there is no problem. Knowing how I arrived at my conclusions, you also know precisely where you disagree with me. You can therefore readily make the necessary changes to incorporate your own views. In either case, you can then proceed to put your capital to work with conviction. By knowing precisely why you are doing what you are doing, you will discover that you won't get upset every time the market moves against you. With logic on your side, you know that sooner or later—and very often sooner—things will come out your way.

Of course, new developments will invariably render some of your assumptions invalid. But again, knowing the specific input for your analysis, you know exactly where adjustments have to be made.

For instance, in my economic study, I already assume that federal spending will increase sharply in the years ahead. As a result, the fiscal deficit in the late 1970's may well exceed an annual rate of $100 billion. That's more than most economists now consider to be even remotely possible. But if Washington really goes haywire and reacts to mounting unemployment by boosting federal spending by, say, another $200 billion, we'll obviously have to modify our economic scenario. That, in turn, will necessitate major revisions in our Flow-of-Funds estimates.

Similarly, if because of some new laws the big banks are proscribed from managing pension funds, the amount and kinds of stocks to be purchased by institutional investors in the future would change drastically. That, too, would require major revisions in our Flow-of-Funds estimates.

Fortunately, these developments don't emerge overnight. By keeping our minds open and alert to changing times, we will have plenty of time to make adjustments. Until and unless new evidence calls for a major reappraisal, meanwhile, we should implement and stick with an investment strategy that is consistent with what we anticipate for the market. Just because we cannot foretell the future with precision is no excuse for living in the past or investing haphazardly.

Let's say you do agree with my current view that bonds will enjoy a long-term upward trend and stocks will undergo a long-term downward trend. It then becomes obvious that one of the safest and soundest ways to build capital in the years ahead is to buy bonds. I use the phrase "to build capital" advisedly. In other words, I think these securities are attractive for purchase not just because they are relatively safe and offer generous income, although these pluses are important. I consider these securities to be interesting capital-building vehicles because I expect them to rise in price over the coming years.

Unfortunately, most investors have little idea how to go about buying bonds. Many "account executives" themselves have limited knowledge of what's happening in the bond market or what changes are taking place in the interest-rate structure.

Actually, the fundamentals of bond investing are quite simple. They encompass only a few elementary rules and definitions.

A bond is essentially a long-term IOU issued by a corporation, the U.S. Treasury or a government agency. When new bonds are offered, the issuer is in effect borrowing from the investing public on certain specified terms. The buyers are the lenders.

There are just a few major kinds of bonds. A mortgage bond is a security collateralized by specific assets such as real property or capital equipment. When the bond is backed solely by general credit, with no lien on specific assets, it is called a debenture. An income bond is one which pays interest only when the interest is earned. Except for speculative purposes, investors should generally avoid these low-quality issues.

Bonds come in either registered or coupon form. In the former case, the owner, whose name and address are recorded with the issuer, receives his interest checks directly from the issuer. A coupon bond is negotiable and is owned by the bearer, who collects his semi-annual interest by literally cutting out a coupon and presenting it to specific banks.

Whereas a shareholder in a corporation is a part owner, the bondholder is a creditor. As a result, he does not share in the future growth of the corporation; but neither does he assume the risks of capital and/or income loss resulting from earnings declines and dividend cuts. And should the company become insolvent, he has a prior claim on assets over the equity holders.

The exact terms of a bond issue—interest rates, maturity date, rights of the holder in case of default, and so on—are spelled out in detail in the indenture executed by the company and the trustees. But just as shareholders do not always have to read the bylaws and corporate minutes of the companies they own, the bond buyers do not usually have to be familiar with all the fine print in the indenture—especially if they restrict their holdings to high-grade issues.

Most bonds are rated by independent organizations, the two best known of which are Moody's and Standard & Poor's. They assess risks against earning power, resources, capital structure, and property protection. Moody's ratings range from Aaa, Aa, and A down through C; Standard & Poor's, from AAA to C. These ratings are not always reliable. In early 1975, for example, when New York's Urban Development Corp. defaulted on its bonds, the issue was rated "A" by Standard & Poor's. But by and large, the bond rating firms try to do a conscientious job on the basis of available information.

Besides the name of the issuer, the two key identifications of a bond are the original interest rate and its maturity date. Take, for instance, General Electric 5.30's, 5/1/92, which are traded on the New York Stock Exchange. Rated Aaa by Moody's and Standard & Poor's, this issue thus pays 5.3% interest and matures on May 1, 1992.

Note that the 5.3% applies to the par value, which for all bonds is $1,000. Thus, the holder of each of these GE bonds will receive $53 a year in interest through May 1, 1992—regardless of how much he originally paid for the bond or where the current quotation is. Actually, interest payments on bonds are almost always made semi-annually—the day and month of the maturity date and exactly six months later. So, the holder of this issue receives $26.50 twice a year. Then, come May 1, 1992, he will be paid by General Electric the $1,000 principal; the bonds will have been redeemed.

Some bonds may be redeemed, or called, by the issuer before maturity. (Many of the high-interest issues sold in recent years, however, have a non-callable provision for at least the first five years. The provision is included to ensure investors receiving the lush income during the non-callable period even in the event interest rates drop sharply.) The call price is typically somewhat higher than the par value.

On the other hand, many bonds have a "sinking fund" provision which requires the issuer to redeem before final maturity a specific number of outstanding bonds annually. This provision is to minimize the danger of the issuer failing to retire the issue at maturity.

Although bonds have a par value of $1,000 each, they are quoted in terms of $100. Hence, a quote of $100 means a bond is selling for $1,000; $104 means it sells for $1040; $68 means $680; and so on.

The commission involved in buying and selling bonds has always been much less than for common stocks. The minimum NYSE commission on a bond selling for over $10 and under $100 was $1.25—before negotiated rates went into effect May 1, 1975. But $1,000 to buy 100 shares of a $10 stock involved a $27.50 commission.

Figuring the yield on a bond of any sort is not too complicated. The current yield is calculated the same way as for common stocks: the annual interest is divided by the market price. However, since a bond is to be redeemed at par value when it reaches maturity, it's more realistic, if the security is selling at a discount (below par), to add to the current yield an amount representing the prorated potential increase in value.

Let's take the case of a bond with a fixed 5% interest rate, maturing in exactly 10 years, and currently selling at $90 ($900 per bond). Since the bond pays an annual interest of $50, its *current yield* is about 5.5% ($50 divided by $900). The bondholder, however, is also assured of a 10-point ($100) capital gain if he holds the issue to maturity, since the company will redeem it at par ($1,000). Prorating the *appreciation to maturity* of roughly 11% over the life of the bond and adding it to the current yield will give the *yield to maturity*. Compound interest is involved here, but the math has all been done and it can easily be determined from a bond table that the yield to maturity in this case is 6.4%.

If a bond is selling at a premium over par, it has a built-in *depreciation to maturity*. In this case, the yield to maturity will be lower than the current yield as well as lower than the coupon rate. Thus, a hypothetical 8% bond, maturing in 10 years, and selling at 120, provides a current yield of 6.7% ($80 divided by $1,200) and a yield to maturity of 5.4%.

Although bonds if held to maturity will always return the full face value to the holder (the danger of default is negligible with high-grade issues), capital gains or losses can indeed result in the interim. This is especially true with issues with long maturities; not everyone can outlive his holdings.

Going bond prices are directly related to prevailing interest rates. Where the bond's annual interest payment is less than the prevailing rates of similar issues and the maturity date is far in the future, it will sell at a discount from par. The reason is that the fixed-interest rates of these bonds are unattractive in the current money market. This means that investors who had originally bought the issues at or near par now have a paper loss.

By the same token, once interest rates in general turn downward, long-term bond prices will advance. Issues with high fixed-interest rates will tend to sell at a premium and those with lower interest rates will go at a smaller discount from par than is presently the case.

Such a decline in interest rates, of course, is precisely why I think bonds should be bought now for capital growth as well as income.

At this point, you probably know almost as much about bonds as your broker. But you still have to decide which issues to buy. Fortunately, this is not nearly as complicated as picking an equity issue. As creditors, bondholders are not affected much by an issuing company's changing fortune; their investments are jeopardized only if the borrower is in serious financial plight. Thus, current earnings and dividends are of minor significance. Instead, the market price is determined largely by prevailing interest-rate conditions and the quality of the bond.

Naturally, a poorly rated bond entails more risk than a top-rated issue of similar terms; hence, it will sell at a lower price. Since bond experts at major financial institutions are constantly monitoring the relative value of individual issues, free-market forces themselves tend to prevent any one issue from being significantly overpriced or underpriced at any given time. Minor aberrations, however, do exist and offer the alert investor some advantage.

But assuming that most issues are on the whole fairly priced, you should make your decisions on the basis of 1) what quality grade you are willing to settle for, 2) what current income you find satisfactory, and 3) how long a maturity date you want.

Within the economic environment I foresee, most bonds rated A or higher are reasonably safe. But a little common sense also

THE HOLT INVESTMENT ADVISORY

MONTHLY FEATURE

Evaluation of Selected Government and Listed Bonds

THE THREE SHADED COLUMNS below represent the prime guides for selecting bonds. The stress to be placed on each column depends on the investor's specific objective: Those seeking maximum current income should choose the bonds within the desired quality group that show the highest **Current Yields**. Generally speaking, issues with high coupon rates and long maturities are likely to give the largest current return. . .Investors prepared to hold bonds until maturity, however, should place greater emphasis on the **Yield to Maturity** column. This figure is a composite of both current yield and appreciation to maturity. Note that bonds with larger appreciation to maturity typically provide smaller current yields. They are particularly suitable for investors in higher tax brackets. . .Finally, the column headed **Potential Appreciation if Yield to Maturity Drops 1%** is of importance to those who wish to capitalize on an intermediate-term decline in interest rates. It shows how much any given issue will rise if its yield to maturity drops 1% point. (Conversely, this column also reveals the approximate downside risk if a general rise in interest rates pushes the bond's yield-to-maturity upward by 1% point.)

Description	Recent Price	Current Yield	Appreciation to Maturity	Yield to Maturity	If Yield to Maturity Drops 1% Bond Price	Potential Apprec.	Call Price (nearest dollar)
U. S. Governments							
U. S. Treasury 3 1/2s, 1980†	83-30	4.2%	19%	7.2%	88.0	4.8%	NC
U. S. Treasury 3 1/4s, 1983-78†	81	4.0%	23%	6.3%	86.7	7.0%	NC till '78
U. S. Treasury 3 1/4s, 1985†	80-30	4.0%	24%	5.8%	87.8	8.5%	100
U. S. Treasury 4 1/4s, 1985-75†	82-12	5.2%	21%	6.7%	89.0	8.0%	100
U. S. Treasury 3 1/2s, 1990†	81	4.3%	23%	5.4%	90.4	11.6%	100
U. S. Treasury 4 1/4s, 1992-87†	81-12	5.2%	23%	6.0%	91.4	12.3%	NC till '87

This is a sample of how The Holt Investment Advisory regularly evaluates selected government and high quality corporate bonds.

comes in handy. After the economy has slowed for years, many of those consumers and businesses which have overextended themselves will have problems paying their bills. Thus, major retail and finance companies that have been extending easy credit to millions of customers across the country will find it difficult getting paid, especially if the average account is small relative to the cost of collection. Hence, no matter how high the bonds of such companies are rated, avoid them.

If you plan to hold the bonds to maturity, both the current yield and the maturity date must, of course, suit your needs. But since the prime reason I think you should buy bonds now is to anticipate declining interest rates, you should select issues that will appreciate most when that materializes.

As a general rule, bonds with distant maturities will be more desirable for this purpose. In a period of declining interest rates, an issue that guarantees the holder a lush return for decades is obviously more sought after than one which matures five years hence.

At times, however, bonds maturing between five to ten years hence will be more suitable. Whereas long-term interest rates tend to follow a slow but sure trend, short- and medium-term rates often fluctuate quite widely in response to economic conditions. There is not much capital growth potential in short-term securities. But at those junctures where medium-term rates are expected to tumble, intermediate-term bonds should certainly be considered for good-sized capital growth.

When interest rates drop across the board, bonds that are currently selling at a lower yield to maturity tend to rise more than one with a higher yield to maturity. This may sound strange since the former appears more dearly priced already. But let me explain.

Let's assume that long-term interest rates will decline 2% across the board over the next couple of years. A fairly priced bond with a 10% yield to maturity will then rise so that it eventually sells on an 8% basis; whereas another fairly priced issue now selling at 7% will rise to sell on a 5% basis. Thus, the yield to maturity of the former will drop 20%, while that of the latter will drop close to 30%. Conversely, the market price of the higher-yield issue will rise less in percentage.

Moreover, bonds selling at lower yields to maturity at present are obviously regarded by the market as having a higher quality and involving fewer risks than those at higher yields. As business activities slow and slow, investors are likely to place increasing emphasis on safety. As a result, they may be willing to pay even larger premiums for high-quality issues than at present. Put another way, the price spread between the top-grade and lesser-grade issues will widen.

Summing up, I am convinced that the time has come to buy bonds for profits. The days of accelerating inflation and ever-rising interest rates are over. As a general rule, investors should consider mostly issues with blue-ribbon qualities. But apply some common sense to supplement the rating services. Also, be flexible about how much capital to put into these securities as well as what maturity bonds to buy. And always, keep a close watch on general market conditions and on the availability of better investment opportunities elsewhere.

CHAPTER 19

Just Take Your Pick

APPLYING THE RULE of thumb I offered at the end of the last chapter, it's become apparent that U.S. Treasury issues are quite suitable for our purposes. There is no doubt whatsoever that obligations of the U.S. Government, backed as they are by the monstrous federal taxing power, are at the top of any list of low-risk instruments.

Remember, however, that new offerings by the Treasury will keep mounting in the coming years. In the not too distant future, the U.S. budget deficit will probably top $100 billion a year. True, I don't expect the government to have much difficulty financing that gap; commercial banks and oil-exporting countries alone can absorb most of the securities offered. But the ever-increasing supply of government issues may mitigate against their appreciating as robustly as prime corporate issues that are in shorter supply. However, for those bond buyers who want maximum safety, this is a relatively small sacrifice to make.

On the credit side, some long-term Treasury bonds have one extra attraction. They can be applied to settle estate taxes at 100, even though most of them are currently selling at hefty discounts from par. For investors with huge estates, this feature is potentially worth a lot of money. The following are in this category:

4 1/4 % May 15, 1975-85
3 1/4 % June 15, 1978-83
4 % Feb. 15, 1980
3 1/2 % Nov. 15, 1980
3 1/4 % May 15, 1985
4 1/4 % Aug. 15, 1987-92
4 % Feb. 15, 1988-93
4 1/8 % May 15, 1989-94
3 1/2 % Feb. 15, 1990
3 % Feb. 15, 1995
3 1/2 % Nov. 15, 1998

Partly because of this special feature, these issues usually are more richly priced than other Treasury securities. But again, for the right investor that's a small premium to pay. (Some of the issues are identified by two years. The first year represents the time when the bonds first become callable; the second, the final maturity date.)

Treasury bonds should not be confused with the Government's Series E and Series H saving bonds. Without meaning to be unpatriotic, I must say that under present market conditions, these saving bonds are dreadfully unattractive. If held to maturity (five years for Series E, and ten years for Series H), the return over the period is equivalent to a mere 6% a year. In case of earlier redemption, the effective yields are much lower.

Nor are all other Treasury obligations "bonds." There are three major varieties, the principal difference among them being the length of maturity from the time of issue.

Treasury *bills* usually mature in three to six months, although some have a life of up to one year. Treasury *notes* have maturities of up to seven years. Treasury *bonds* have original maturities of five years and longer, sometimes up to 30 years.

Treasury bills are issued at a discount from par, and the difference between the cost and the face value represents the interest income to the buyer. In periods of high short-term rates, they are excellent income producers. For capital-building purposes, however, issues with longer maturities are where the action is.

Both Treasury notes and bonds are offered at par either for cash or in exchange for outstanding or maturing securities. Typically, offerings are announced ten to twenty days before the date of issue, and the books are open for subscription entries anywhere from one day to a week.

Commercial banks can usually submit bids for their own and customers' accounts. Private subscribers, however, are required to post a deposit with the Federal Reserve or with their own banks—usually 10% for small subscriptions and 2% for those in excess of $200,000. On cash offerings, over-subscription is the norm; but the Treasury makes preferential allotments to certain investor classes, including private individuals.

As noted earlier, Treasury notes are issued with an original maturity of one to seven years, while Treasury bonds generally have an original maturity of well over five years. As far as the private investors are concerned, however, the two types are not significantly different. Being direct obligations of the U.S. Treasury, both are backed by the full taxing power of the Government. Both are traded in $1,000 lots. As a matter of fact, the *Wall Street Journal* and many other dailies usually list quotations of these issues in the same table.

Like corporate bonds, government issues are identified by their interest rates and maturity dates. Thus, U.S. Treasury 3s, 1995 represents an issue with an interest rate of 3% and matures in 1995.

Treasury notes and bonds are available in registered as well as in coupon form. In the case of a registered issue, the name and address of the owner are recorded with the government. This form of ownership gives more protection against theft. (The books at the Treasury Department close for the transfer of registered bonds one month prior to each interest payment date.) A coupon bond, on the other hand, is technically owned by the bearer, whoever he may be. They are more suitable for large institutional investors. Registered and coupon bonds are interchangeable.

Treasury notes are generally noncallable. In other words, they cannot be redeemed at the Government's option prior to maturity. For high coupon issues, this is an important feature. In early 1970, for example, the Treasury issued a seven-year note carrying an 8% rate and maturing February 15, 1977. Holders of this issue have thus been guaranteed 8% per annum income for seven years. Even when interest rates subsequently dropped somewhat, the Treasury could not call those notes and replace them with new ones carrying lower interest.

A few long-term bonds are callable at par a few years before they reach maturity. For example, the $4\frac{1}{4}\%$, August 1987-1992 may be redeemed by the Treasury starting in 1987 even though the issue matures in 1992. In the present money market, however, this call feature is all but meaningless. Most callable bonds are low-coupon issues now selling at hefty discounts from par. Unless long-term interest rates drop well below 4%, which is unlikely in the years immediately ahead, there is no reason whatsoever why the Government would want to retire these issues prematurely.

One of the prime advantages of buying Treasury notes and bonds is that these securities have an active trading market. The dealers and banks that maintain the market in Governments quote prices on a net basis. In other words, on full lots—100 bonds of $100,000 par value—they will pay the bid price and sell at the asked price without commissions.

Investors interested in smaller amounts, however, have to place their orders with their banks or brokers, who usually tack on a small commission. There is no set commission rate since everything is negotiable in the Government bond market. However, a not unusual rate in smaller deals to individuals is $62\frac{1}{2}$c per $1,000 bond—a negligible figure compared with the commissions involved in stock transactions.

Market prices of Government bonds and rates are generally quoted in terms of 32nds. Thus a quotation of 93-8 means 93 8/32, or $93\frac{1}{4}$. Since a quote of 100 equals par, that 93-8 equals $932.50 per $1,000 bond. The settlement day for Government securities transactions is usually the next full business day following the trade.

The quotations published daily by dealers and printed in many newspapers are often accompanied by the yields of the respective notes and bonds. These figures, computed on the asked side of the market—the price the buyer has to pay—represent yields to maturity, which take into consideration potential capital gains (or losses) to maturity as well as current income.

A number of agencies created by the federal government are authorized to sell debt to the investing public. Like Treasury issues, many of these securities can be bought and sold on the open market in $1,000 lots. While such paper and bonds are not direct obligations of the U.S. Government, they're certainly the next best thing, having been accorded quality classifications that rank them next to Treasury securities. All of the issuing agencies were established by acts of Congress, and the government maintains an active interest in them through equity positions and supervisory controls.

As a rule, these agency issues offer somewhat higher returns than Treasury securities. Listed in approximate order of size, the most important agencies are:

Federal Home Loan Bank, which was organized to extend credit to residential mortgage-lending and thrift institutions like savings and loan associations.

Federal Land Banks, a 12-institution system that makes long-term low-interest mortgage loans to farmers through associations.

Federal National Mortgage Association (Fannie Mae), a now quasi-public corporation whose job is to provide a secondary market for mortgages insured by the Federal Housing Administration or guaranteed by the Veterans Administration.

Federal Intermediate Credit Banks, which underwrite the seasonal needs of farmers and stock men in the areas of production and marketing by discounting agricultural loan paper.

Central Bank for Cooperations, which assists agricultural associations by making loans on commodity crops, property, equipment and facilities.

International Bank for Reconstruction & Development (World Bank), which makes loans to developing foreign countries.

These agencies sell their own obligations publicly to secure the funds needed to carry on their activities. As noted earlier, though their securities are not on a par with those of the Treasury, they possess a high degree of marketability. Evidence of their acceptance is apparent in the narrowing spread between their yields and those on direct Treasury obligations.

Agency issues, with the exception of those from the FNMA, are similar to Treasury securities. Interest is fully taxable for federal purposes but exempt from state levies. Interest on Fannie Mae's obligations is fair game for any taxing body.

Daily quotations of these agencies' issues, as well as Treasury securities, are published regularly in the *Wall Street Journal* under the heading: Government, Agency and Miscellaneous Securities.

For those investors who are willing to accept a trifle more risk in exchange for greater capital growth potential as well as higher current income, prime corporate bonds may be more attractive. Like everything else, the price of any bond is affected by the volume of potential supply. The supply of new corporate bonds during the slow economy ahead is bound to be limited. Free-market forces are thus likely to produce prices a bit higher than usual for already outstanding issues.

In this connection, bonds issued by industrial companies will probably be in ever shorter supply than those sold by utilities. Although they have recently slowed down their expansion projects, utilities—which typically map out capital construction programs years and years ahead—will have a continuing need for outside funds. By way of contrast, very few manufacturing firms will find it necessary to raise new debt capital.

(In the economic and market environment I foresee for the remainder of this decade, bonds of transportation companies are generally too risky and should not be purchased to anticipate a downward trend in interest rates. But, as I will discuss later in this book, they are not altogether out of bounds for the Total Investor.)

Having been exposed almost exclusively to common shares, many investors may find investing in bonds terribly dull. In the stock market, it's not unusual for volatile issues to jump 50% or more in a year (although few investors can really buy near the absolute lows and sell near the highs). But for high-grade, long-term bonds to score even a 20% rise in a 12-month period would require an extraordinarily sharp drop in interest rates.

But don't let this relative stability deter you from investing in bonds. Look at it this way. Even if you achieve a capital growth of only 5% a year, your total annual return would well exceed 10%. It's not hard to find top-quality bonds that are currently yielding 7% or more at present. And if you could attain a 10%-plus total annual return consistently, you'd be doing quite a bit better than what those big banks have achieved for their multibillion-dollar pension-fund clients in the past decade.

As a private investor, you can buy bonds on margin. This is another boon for the flexible investor. Many experts say that using margin to buy securities is a no-no for serious investors. But then, these are probably the same experts who consider it perfectly prudent to buy stocks of corporations that are heavily in debt.

For those of you not familiar with the term margin, let me just explain that it involves buying securities partly with borrowed money. Thus, if you put up only $400 of capital to buy a security issue that costs $1,000, borrowing the remaining $600 from your broker or your bank, you are using only 40% margin. Most brokers will open a margin account for you routinely, but you can also borrow from commercial banks. Of course, you must pay interest on the borrowed money; you will also have to let the lender hold your securities as collateral.

Using margin means using leverage. Thus, if you are able to sell the issue in the above example for $1,100, you'd have a profit of $100. While such a profit represents 10% of the $1,000 cost, it is equivalent to 25% of the $400 capital you originally put up.

Leverage, of course, works both ways. A 10% drop in that security would result in a 25% loss in your equity. And if your equity drops too low, your friendly broker or banker will require that you put up additional capital—or he will sell out your collateral. It is this danger that brings added risks to margin investing.

But the increased risk inherent in the use of borrowed money for investing purposes applies also to the use of debt to finance business operations or to buy cars or homes. True, many companies do go bankrupt when things go wrong, and many individuals do lose their personal and real property. Yet without the use of credit the U.S. economy would not have grown into the biggest in the world in just two centuries, and the standard of living here would not now be the highest.

The fact is, of course, that there is nothing wrong whatsoever with the prudent use of debt. That's why, even with their heavy debt loads, companies like AT&T and IBM, Bankamerica and Morgan Stanley are all regarded, even by the fiscal prude, as financially sound.

No businessman knows precisely what the future will bring. To maximize the return on capital, good managements typically develop corporate plans and budgets on the basis of probable economic developments. That is exactly how investment strategies should be mapped. The analysis we went through earlier in this book concluded that bond prices will most probably trend upward in the years ahead. Thus, buying high-grade bonds on margin constitutes a decidedly prudent use of debt.

According to existing margin regulations, Treasury securities may be bought on only 5% margin and straight corporate bonds (as distinguished from convertible bonds) can be bought on as little as 20%-30% margin, depending on the lending institution. Using such low margins would indeed be imprudent inasmuch as an upward trend for bond prices does not preclude interim declines that might result in margin calls. But I see nothing wrong in using, say, 50% margin.

Potentially, there is an additional plus in buying bonds on margin. As the economy softens, short-term interest rates will stand well below long-term rates. When that happens, margin helps to increase current interest income. Let's say you invest $1,000 to buy an 8% bond at par. Your investment yields $80 interest income per annum. But if you use 50% margin and buy two such bonds, your gross interest income would be $160. You'll have to pay interest on the $1,000 you borrow. But if short-term rates are much lower and you only have to pay, say, 5%, your cost is just $50 a year. Net interest income: $110—or a current yield of 11%.

Treasury, agency and corporate bonds are by no means the only fixed income securities available. State and local governments also sell bonds to meet their financial needs. As a matter of fact, many investors in high tax brackets find such securities particularly attractive because the interest they receive is exempt from federal and sometimes state income-tax liability.

This is one group of securities I think investors should avoid, however. Having grown enormously in recent decades, most governments are now too big to be efficiently run. In good times, the shortcomings of oversized bureaucracies are obscured. But from now on, their tax revenues will probably be depressed. Worse yet, the taxpayers' revolt is becoming more intense at the state and local level. As a result, any number of municipal governments will find it increasingly difficult to make ends meet. Their bonds will become bad risks. There will no doubt be some exceptions; but why go to the trouble of looking for these exceptions when so many other investment opportunities are available elsewhere? As I pointed out before, tax considerations should always be subordinated to investment considerations.

The preferred stocks of many strong corporations, on the other hand, are well worth considering. Preferred stocks fall somewhere between corporate debt and traditional equities. Like bond interest payments, the dividend paid by a preferred is fixed. For example, the Virginia Electric and Power $7.45 cumulative preferred, which has a $100 face value, pays $7.45 a year regularly.

Nevertheless, failure to pay a preferred dividend does not automatically constitute a default. In the case of a cumulative preferred, omitted dividends must usually be made up before any payment can be distributed to common shareholders.

While bondholders are creditors, preferred stockholders are owners of the company. But unlike common stockholders, they do not usually vote at the annual meeting. Typically, they can vote only after the preferred dividend is passed for a specific length of time. On the positive side, if the company goes into liquidation or reorganization, preferred stockholders have a prior claim over investors holding the common.

Since I am talking about preferred stock of strong companies (in terms of balance sheet conditions), the difference between preferred stocks and bonds is academic. If the company involved is even remotely in danger of failing, both their bonds and preferred stocks should be avoided anyway.

For investment purposes, high-grade preferred issues possess two special features that are likely to win them heightened popularity in the years ahead. First, while some are callable at or above par, preferred stocks do not mature. In a period of declining interest rates, buying a high-yield issue at a discount from face value is especially attractive. It guarantees the holder the currently high yield indefinitely, a healthy capital gain, or both.

Second, under existing tax laws, 85% of the dividends received by industrial corporations are tax-exempt. In the economic scenario I foresee, many large corporations will have excess cash flow. Their capital expenditures will be minimal. To maximize the after-tax return they earn, many such corporations will invest idle cash in prime preferred stocks. In short, the flow of corporate funds into these securities will become unusually large.

By discussing preferred stocks as well as Treasury, U.S. agency and corporate bonds in this chapter, and by explaining the use of margin, I hope you'll begin to get a better feel for the Total Investment approach. You can see now how investors can use a variety of securities, and why it makes sense to be flexible. In the next few chapters, I shall explore this approach further.

CHAPTER 20

How to Have Fun in a Bear Market

NOW, LET'S LOOK at the stock market. Here, our Flow-of-Funds study reveals that a downward price trend will probably develop in the years ahead.

In the wake of both the 1969-70 and the 1973-74 market declines, literally hundreds of investors told me: "I should have listened to you." They, of course, had failed to get out of stocks in time. While I wish they had listened to me, I can well understand why they resisted. I did not always have the opportunity to explain in detail all the reasons and assumptions behind my investment recommendations; so, for many, my minority view was hard to accept. Besides, investors have in recent years been taking the advice of every expert with a heavy dose of salt.

But before those two market breaks, I heard the following remark with equal frequency: "What you said makes good sense, but I hope you're wrong." In fact, I am hearing the very same broken record currently in the summer of 1975. This is something I have found hard to understand. Why do so many people refuse to face up to reality?

Even a child has enough common sense not to go out in his best suit without an umbrella or a raincoat when the weather forecast calls for an approaching storm. And heaven knows how wrong weather forecasters can be. Yet, when it comes to their hard-earned savings, many otherwise intelligent people let their personal emotions overcome their best judgment.

Obviously, most investors don't want a bear market because declining stock prices mean shrinking value for their stock holdings. But what they want and what is in prospect are two different things. What these investors ignore is the fact that stocks can be sold. No one is required to hold on to his equity investments and ride the bear market all the way down. Why not think positively and regard a bear market as a healthy development enabling us to buy the stocks we want at better prices later?

Earlier in this book, I explained why allowing investment capital to be locked in by gains, losses or whatever is bad investment practice. I also explained why the Total Investor should practice the Kung Fu principle—converting adverse forces into positive, productive power. Instead of fearing an approaching bear market, therefore, we should use it to build capital.

With that in mind, it is obvious that one safe and sure way to protect and build capital in a bear market is to sell short.

To many, that statement may sound irresponsible. But once you think it through, you should agree that under bear-market conditions, selling short is a conservative investment approach.

Because conventional wisdom has given short selling such a horrifying image, most investors probably don't even bother to know what it's all about. Actually, it merely involves selling a security not currently owned with the hope of buying it back later at a lower price.

Thus, if you come across a stock way overpriced, one that is clearly headed downward, you may find it advisable to sell it now and buy it back later. Thus, if you can sell that stock at 50 and then repurchase it at only 20, you would have a profit of 30 points. Of course, if the stock goes up and you have repurchased it at 80, you would end up with a 30-point loss.

When the initial short sale is made, the stock has to be borrowed from a current owner so that delivery can be made to the investor who buys it from you. This borrowing process sounds complicated. But it is really a simple matter routinely handled by most brokerage firms through a few accounting entries. As a matter of fact, chances are the real owner doesn't even know his stock has been lent to you. (Brokers do have permission from margin account customers to effect such lending, however.)

The short position is subsequently closed out, or "covered," when the stock involved is finally repurchased and returned to the lender. As you can see, selling short is just a simple reversal of the normal buy-and-then-sell sequence.

Nevertheless, the conventional wisdom regards short selling as something wicked. It is un-American, they say. Its success depends on terrible things happening to the economy. It adds to the downward pressure in a bear market. Reflecting this view, there is even a law requiring that a short sale be made only at a price higher than the last different price.

The sinister image of short selling actually originated back in the early 1930's when unscrupulous financiers conspired to drive selected stocks sharply downward by shorting enormous numbers of shares. Such manipulation obviously cannot be tolerated. But to conclude that selling short, *per se,* is therefore evil is not unlike condemning all investing just because some manipulators illegally drive a few stocks upward.

Once emotion is put aside, one can readily see why there is nothing wrong in short selling. It is, if anything, an important stabilizing force in the free market. In commodities and foreign exchange dealings, short sales are regularly executed by reputable corporations and government agencies. On the floor of the stock exchanges, it is a function required of stock specialists.

Looking back over the past decade, I think a case can be made that the market has suffered from insufficient short selling. In 1967-68, for instance, many performance-oriented mutual funds were chasing after thinly capitalized stocks of questionable value. As a result, many low-grade issues skyrocketed in price, attracting millions of private investors in the process.

The subsequent collapse of those "go-go" stocks resulted in untold billions of dollars of losses for the unsuspecting public.

Had there been more short selling by private traders as well as by specialists who are supposed to maintain an orderly market, the initial upsurge and the subsequent collapse would both have been substantially moderated.

Similarly, had there been more short selling by both the public and the stock exchange specialists in 1972-73, the big banks would not have been able to drive their favorite glamour stocks so sharply upward, and the steep drop that followed would also have been avoided. In other words, pension funds would not have lost the tens of billions of dollars they did lose, thereby jeopardizing the welfare of millions of participants.

Because short selling creates an added supply of stocks when demand is excessive, and the subsequent covering results in added buying when demand is low, it mitigates sharp price rises and falls, and thereby strengthens the free-market system. It is certainly not un-American.

After a short sale is made, the investor does expect the stock shorted to come down. But his decision to sell short to begin with was obviously motivated by the prospect of a bear market. No one blames umbrella salesmen for approaching rainstorms. Why condemn short sellers for anticipating an approaching bear market?

Even if it is not morally wrong, some critics say, short selling is extremely risky. It involves unfavorable odds. Mathematically, the critics are right. A stock can multiply in price many, many times but it can never decline more than 100%. Hence, selling short can theoretically result in infinite losses, but can never generate more than a 100% profit.

But this theory fails to take into consideration such important factors as the stock's relative value and technical condition, overall economic developments, and the market's underlying trend. The Total Investor does consider all these factors.

Moreover, it is undeniable that in a bear market, stocks are more likely to go down than up. In the final analysis, probabilities—not theoretical possibilities—determine investment risks and rewards.

"But how can anyone who sells short consider himself an investor?" the critic may ask. Why not? According to Webster's

Dictionary, to "invest" is to commit money in order to earn a financial return. This is precisely what selling short in a bear market aims to do.

What many people have forgotten is that the stock market is merely a vehicle with which to build capital. It doesn't make sense for investors to use a vehicle going only one way and not the other. If anything, the trouble in recent years is that too many investors have tried to go uptown on a downtown bus.

But what's the use of debating? The effectiveness of short selling in building capital can best be illustrated by the actual record of The Holt Investment Advisory. The Advisory first recommended outright short selling in September 1971, shortly after President Nixon decided to impose wage and price controls. The market had responded to the "imaginative" New Economic Program by roaring sharply upward. We continued to make short sale recommendations thereafter through June 1974. All shorts were then covered by September of that year. (We followed essentially the same policy during that period for our Strategic Money Management clients who allowed us to sell short.)

In that three-year period, the Advisory made 46 specific short-sale recommendations. Of that total, only 2 sustained a loss; the other 44 resulted in profits. Our batting average: .956.

For the entire 46 shorts, the average gain was 37.5%. That, I submit, is investing with a capital "I." It sure beats losing money in a bear market.

For those who are convinced that selling short is a low-risk way to build capital in a bear market, let me present the following guidelines:

1) *Don't buck the primary trend.* Many inexperienced investors are tempted to short those stocks that have just skyrocketed on the assumption that such stocks must be overpriced. But frequently, sudden market strength is followed by announcements of sharply increased earnings and dividends or other unexpected developments that increase the underlying value of the stock. Moreover, many investors, including major institutions, have a habit of zeroing their capital in on the few issues that are in the limelight. Until such buyers have exhausted their resources, overpriced stocks often become more and more overpriced.

2) *Don't short thin issues.* Stocks with small floating supplies tend to flucutate erratically. These issues could indeed tumble steeply in a bear market. If manipulators decide to pool their resources and buy up the floating supply, short sellers could find themselves unable to repurchase the borrowed stocks without paying fabulous prices.

3) *Don't short stocks with large assets.* As the bear market progresses, many stocks will sell at substantial discounts from their asset values. Companies rich in liquid assets could become takeover candidates. A surprise merger offer or liquidation announcement could cause these issues to jump sharply.

4) *Don't short stocks paying large dividends.* Unless there are sound reasons to expect an imminent dividend cut, stocks with very large payouts should be avoided. A safe and generous yield often provides a floor for the stock, especially since investors typically switch emphasis from growth to income in a bear market.

5) *Don't get impatient.* Like buying stocks long, short selling them can be designed to trade against near-term fluctuations or capitalize on longer-term trends. I don't think anyone should try to catch the short-term cycles—either on the long or short side. It involves costly commissions and is nerve-wracking as well.

Capitalizing on longer-term trends, on the other hand, entails much less risk; changes in these trends can usually be anticipated with accuracy. But such trends unfold slowly. The short-selling investor must therefore be prepared to hold the position for up to two or three years, if necessary.

6) *Don't overextend yourself.* To be flexible, you should vary the portion of your portfolio allocated to outright short sales. Try to practice the theory of contrary opinion by shorting more heavily when the mass is confident, reducing your shorts when the mass is turning worried, and covering your positions altogether when the mass is panicking. But at any rate, do not apply more than 50% of your portfolio to selling short. This will protect you from margin calls if your shorts run against you temporarily.

7) *Short has-been glamours.* On their way up, glamour issues with high price-earnings ratios should be avoided. But once these stocks top out they become highly suitable short candidates. This

is especially true of companies that have passed their earnings growth peak. It is not necessary for earnings comparisons actually to turn unfavorable. For overpriced shares, the mere fact that the earnings growth rate is visibly slowing is usually sufficient to cause sharp declines.

8) *Monitor institutional transactions.* In recent years, funds managed by the big banks have been one of the most disruptive forces in the stock market. Impatient buying or dumping has resulted in violent price movements. It is possible to make use of this force by shorting those stocks which are heavily held by such funds and which are beginning to be unloaded by them. Though a few months after the fact, this information regularly appears in financial publications like *Barron's.*

9) *Update your evaluation.* Any investment position, whether long or short, must be continually reviewed. In the case of short selling, it is all the more important for you to ascertain at all times that the reasoning behind the original action is still valid. If things go wrong, take losses if necessary and use the capital elsewhere. Never, never be stubborn.

10) *Stick with your conviction.* Conversely, if you are reasonably sure that your analysis is right, don't let temporary reverses upset your judgment. Remember, for short periods of time the market can be quite irrational. The stocks you've shorted for the right reason could go up against you from time to time. But as long as a primary bear market is underway, that stock will eventually succumb to free-market forces.

With those ten guidelines, I think you should be able to have some fun in the coming bear market.

Incidentally, because short selling involves borrowing stocks from the broker, it cannot be effected in a regular cash account. A short account and a margin account have to be opened. Since most brokerage firms send out one statement for each of these accounts, some short-selling investors receive several statements each month as a result.

But it is not difficult to evaluate one's portfolio, the many statements notwithstanding. Typically, the last figure on the right side of each statement, represents the debit or credit balance of that account. And the "security position" on the lower part of the statement shows the name and amount of each security owned (long) or borrowed (short).

To find the current market value of your entire portfolio, first determine the market value of all stocks and bonds held (the long position). Add to that figure credit balances, if any, for the various accounts. Then deduct the debt balances, if any. Finally, deduct the market value of all borrowed securities (the short position). The remainder represents the current market value of your portfolio.

All this may sound terribly confusing to you, I know. But it's not really that bad. Once you have the actual statements in front of you, the last two paragraphs will make much more sense.

Before I leave this subject, I must point out also that many brokerage firms do not charge interest for lending you the stock to short. But whenever the company pays a dividend, you will have to pay it. Why? Let's say you borrowed a stock from A and sold it to B. When the company pays its dividend, the check is sent to B, the shareholder of record. But A still owns the stock, so you have to reimburse him for the dividend due him.

If you concentrate on shorting overpriced stocks that have no or little current yields, your borrowing costs will be quite low. But there is an added kicker here. After you make your short sale, your account is credited for the proceeds. The money you have to put up to support the transaction represents a credit balance in your margin account. As a result, you will have a very large credit balance on the asset side and the borrowed stock on the debit side. You cannot withdraw the money. But some brokers will allow you to use some or all of that credit balance to buy short-term Treasury bills which, for all practical purposes, are riskless. As a result, you'll be earning interest on the capital applied to support your short sale. That's one way of having your cake and eating it too.

CHAPTER 21

The Long End of It

THE LAST CHAPTER notwithstanding, I'm sure many readers will still find it difficult to live with short selling. To them the fear of selling short is too ingrained to be removed. If you are one of them, don't feel bad; just forego short selling altogether. This is one case where we have to be flexible in being flexible.

Good investment results come only from a program with which you are fully at ease and in which you have strong conviction.

Moreover, even in a long-term bear market, there are times when selling short is not advisable. Although the last primary bull market ended back in late 1968, for example, I did not consider it safe to start shorting until late 1971. All outstanding shorts were then covered in the fall of 1974. As of this writing, my Flow-of-Funds analysis indicates that the next appropriate time will come in the summer of 1975.

Fortunately, this does not mean that you have to forego the equity market altogether. In the years ahead, excellent investment opportunities will inevitably emerge on the long side from time to time. To be sure, to make full use of these opportunities, your timing will have to be sharper and your judgment keener. More than ever, you must learn to stay one step ahead of the crowd. So, be fully prepared to take and maintain a minority position. It's not easy. But if you do succeed in making money on the long side in a bear market, your satisfaction will be that much greater.

In a bear market, profit opportunities are most abundant by far when stocks are deeply oversold and when a major secondary recovery is imminent.

Let me stress that by "deeply oversold," I mean *really* deeply oversold. Brokers and market commentators have a habit of describing the market as oversold whenever it has undergone a sinking spell for a few weeks or every time the Dow average tumbles 40 or 50 points. But in a primary bear market, that is the norm. The technical recoveries that follow such normal declines are more often than not feeble and short-lived. A *really* deeply oversold condition arrives only when pessimism is all but universal and when brokers and market commentators no longer talk about an imminent recovery.

To illustrate my point, let's look at how stock prices have behaved since the current primary bear market started. Because such popularly watched averages as the Dow-Jones industrials and the New York Stock Exchange composite are distorted by their blue-chip components, the accompanying chart shows the Value Line Composite. This average, computed by Arnold Bernhard & Co. of New York, is based on, and gives equal weight to, over 1,500 stocks. It provides a better picture of the market in general.

Note that from late 1968 until mid-1970 and again from the spring of 1972 to late 1974, the market retreat was interrupted by only minor recoveries. With the exception of the very alert, those investors who tried to catch such interim rallies either ended up paying lots of commissions to their brokers while realizing little or no profit, or got caught in the subsequent decline.

On the other hand, the recoveries that started in the middle of 1970 and in late 1974 both lasted half a year or more, and both generated substantial percentage gains. The 1970-71 rise boosted the Value Line Composite by some 45%, the 1974-75 rally some

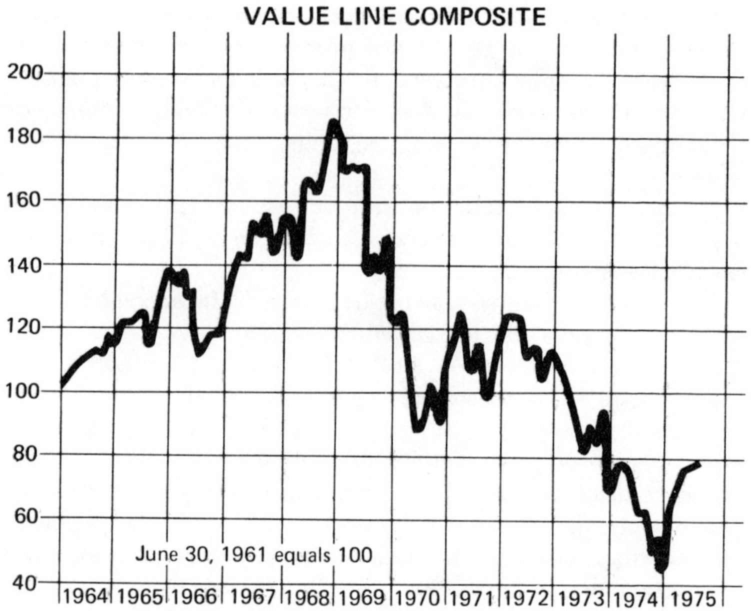

The Value Line Composite, an unweighted index based on over 1,500 stocks, reveals that since the primary bear market started in late 1968, there were only two significant recoveries. One started in mid-1970, the other in late 1974.

65% (as of mid-1975). These are the interim advances in which investors can participate without exposing themselves to too much risk.

But are these substantial rallies recognizable only after the fact? Not at all. Here again, the Flow-of-Funds analytical approach comes in handy. To help differentiate fleeting rallies from sustained advances, let's review again what primary, secondary and tertiary market trends are.

In terms of time, a primary trend is one that persists for years or even decades; a secondary one usually goes on for several months, but occasionally as long as a couple of years; and a tertiary trend lasts from a few days to a few months. By this definition, the nature of any given trend is indeed recognizable only after the fact.

The Flow-of-Funds study, however, identifies the three market trends in a different manner. As I pointed out in an earlier chapter, private investors own the great majority of common stocks as well as the bulk of liquid financial assets. Collectively, they exercise strong control over the supply of and the demand for stocks. Their equity transactions, in short, are the dominant influence on the market's underlying trend.

When private investors—motivated by rising savings, strengthening confidence, attractive yields from equities, or whatever—put an increasing amount of funds into the market, they stash away their stocks. The active demand thus increases while the active supply is diminishing. Result: a primary bull market.

Conversely, if more and more investors sell off their long-term, stashed-away equity holdings, money is withdrawn from the market and the active supply increases. Unless that increased supply is offset by institutional buying, a primary bear market emerges.

The secondary trend, on the other hand, is governed by the flow of those funds controlled by the generally more sophisticated—though not necessarily the more successful. These investors, whether individuals or institutions, turn over their portfolios more actively than long-term investors, though they do not trade on a day-to-day or a week-to-week basis.

Whereas most private investors have but a superficial understanding of business conditions, this "informed" group responds keenly to economic, monetary and company developments. For that reason, these secondary market trends tend to correspond with business cycles—or, more precisely, with how these investors interpret and react to "fundamental" developments.

Tertiary market trends are attributable to the flow of those funds controlled by active speculating traders. Strangely, like long-term investors, these traders are not economy-minded. They move in and out of the market actively regardless of business conditions, depending mainly on charts and other technical indicators. But unlike the serious investors, they do react violently—and usually erroneously—to late-breaking business news.

Knowing these important differences, you'll find that differentiating the substantial recoveries that started in mid-1970 and in late 1974 from the many fleeting bear-market flurries was not all that difficult. As a matter of fact, the approach of those major rallies could be well anticipated.

To be more specific, our Flow-of-Funds analysis reveals that most of the technical rallies during those bear markets were traceable to temporary influxes of trading money controlled by in-and-out speculators. By way of contrast, in the spring of 1970 and again in the fall of 1974, there was a conspicuous inflow of investment funds from long-term private investors. Moreover, shortly after those two specific recoveries had gotten underway, the inflow of "sophisticated" money into the stock market also increased markedly.

There is no way to tell at this point just when the next substantial bear-market advance will begin. Chances are, however, that it will come only after stock prices have first undergone another substantial and protracted decline. Before it occurs, the Total Investor should have on hand ample buying power to capitalize on the move. Until then, therefore, keep a good portion of your investment assets liquid.

Just as a major bear-market rally typically starts when pessimism is prevalent, it usually ends when Wall Streeters are overconfident. Investors wishing to take advantage of major bear-market advances must therefore be prepared to take profits just when things looks especially rosy.

This is easier said than done. All too often in recent years many investors did manage to buy bargains near the market bottom. But they subsequently overstayed the rally because there was so much bullishness around. As a result, their stock subsequently dropped to levels well below the original bargain prices. So, no matter what the prevailing Wall Street views are, don't forget that we are still in a primary bear market.

Which stocks should one buy when the next bear-market rally comes? Anyone who gives you a specific answer to that question is a pseudo-expert. Nobody knows now which stocks will sell at which price at that point.

But here is something to keep in mind. The next secondary advance will get underway only after—and because—private individuals are buying stocks on balance again. Chances are that buying will be reinforced shortly thereafter by increased institutional purchases. Generally speaking, private individuals like to buy stocks of well known companies that have fallen sharply and that offer attractive current yields. Financial institutions, meanwhile, tend to buy blue-chip issues with large capitalizations. These are prime areas, then, where the alert investor should look for possible bargains.

In bear-market rallies, there will always be some "cats and dogs" that double or triple in price—if only because they have previously suffered exceptionally sharp nosedives. But don't try to catch these issues in the next secondary advance. For every one that does soar, there may be a score that sink to still lower levels. In a protracted economic slump, the number of marginal firms that become insolvent can skyrocket. Moreover, the risk of overstaying even the winners is great. Low-quality stocks with limited capitalizations can plummet as fast as they catapult.

Except during periods of panic selling, some selected stocks will probably be able to buck the bear market from time to time. Again, for me to give specific examples now would imply that the stocks selected are attractive at any price. Nothing is. But once more, some common-sense guidelines can be useful.

For instance, we expect interest rates to decline generally over the coming years. If so, interest-sensitive equities may very well appreciate along with bonds and preferred stocks. What are interest-sensitive stocks? Those that pay a steady dividend—a dividend that is not jeopardized by the slow economy. Many utilities, food and petroleum companies may fall into this group. Make sure, however, that their current yields are generous, compared with other investment vehicles as well as with their own past norms.

The economic scenario I foresee also incorporates ever increasing spending by the federal government to support the economy. I don't expect such efforts to really succeed. But those industries which are immediate recipients of government expenditures should do relatively well. Some of the companies related to aerospace, energy, sewer treatment, public works, mass transit equipment and the like might be considered. But don't buy stocks in these industries unthinkingly. Make sure that the companies you buy are financially strong and well-managed. More importantly, make sure that the stocks are capable of providing generous yields and that prospective government business could result in still higher dividends.

My economic scenario also calls for an official gold price of about $200 an ounce in the 1980's. Such a development may help lift the price of silver above $7.50 an ounce. Precious metal companies which can generate good dividend-paying power from such product prices may also be among the maverick stocks in the coming bear market.

Because there is so much confusion surrounding the merits (or demerits) of precious metal issues, I believe some elaboration on this subject is in order.

Most Americans probably do not give much thought to gold. But those who do typically fall into two emotionally extreme groups. The first hold the "barbarous metal" in contempt, regarding it as something poisonous to the economy. The other group idolizes gold, considering an investment in the metal a panacea for both runaway inflation and ultra-deflation.

Why do some people have such strong feelings on this subject? The discussion of the world monetary situation earlier in this book actually provides the answer. When gold represented the foundation for both the domestic and international monetary structures, it served to limit credit expansion at home and the outflow of dollars abroad. Since liberal economic and political policies can only be implemented with the help of unlimited credit expansion and continuing payments deficits, those favoring such policies cannot help but regard gold as an economic and political foe.

By the same token, economists and politicians with conservative leanings naturally favor retention of gold as a disciplinary force. I put myself among the latter group.

I do not consider gold or gold shares a perfect investment at all times, however. For my firm's investment clients, I have maintained substantial positions in precious metal issues for years. But these shares will not be held indefinitely. At some point, profits will be taken. The fact is, even gold and gold stocks cannot be a good buy at any price.

The reason why many advisors have considered investment in

gold bullion and gold shares a heads-I-win-tails-you-lose proposition is easy to find. The metal is indeed a hedge against a runaway inflation. The more governments print paper monies and the more those paper monies depreciate in value, the more will worldwide demand for gold develop. Many people outside the United States do instinctively turn to gold as a store of value, especially during troubled times.

But these same experts also favor gold in a depression, mainly because gold acted well back in the 1930's. Then, widespread deflation notwithstanding, the price of gold was raised by President Roosevelt. And despite the general collapse in stock prices, gold mining shares soared.

But one reason why gold stocks managed to buck the 1929-32 market crash was because they had hardly gone up in the 1920's. Similarly, before deflation hit in the early 1930's, the price of gold had not advanced. The then official rate of $20.67 per ounce was hardly challenged.

It was only in late 1932 and early 1933—after stock and commodity prices had already plummeted dramatically—that the dollar became suspect. Moreoever, gold shares underwent their astronomical rise mainly in 1933 and that was the year commodity and stock prices were recovering from their previous tumble, the year when President Roosevelt raised the official gold price and began to debase the dollar.

The situation is quite different now. Deflation hasn't really started yet, but the price of gold has already multiplied in the last several years. And most precious metal stocks have so far bucked the bear market by rising from their 1960's levels.

If inflation continues on and on and the purchasing power of fiat money goes down and down, there's no telling how high gold and allied precious metals can go. But we have already established earlier that the long-term credit expansion cycle is coming to an end and deflation may soon take hold in this country. Such a scenario is not conducive to an ever rising gold price.

Why, then, should investors even consider investing in precious metal stocks during the coming bear market? I can see two reasons:

1) Until deflation becomes highly conspicuous, most people

throughout the world, having lived with inflation for generations, will continue to think in terms of hedging against inflation. Most governments are now sustaining heavy fiscal deficits and people automatically equate mounting fiscal deficits with inflation. For that reason, I foresee at least one giant wave of gold buying developing in 1976 or 1977, when the depreciation of most foreign currencies becomes conspicuous. The price of both bullion and gold mining shares will then almost certainly jump sharply. (That will probably be the ideal time to take profits.)

2) I expect the next world monetary reform to peg the price of gold officially around the $200 level—at a time when the free-market quotation will have dropped considerably from the gold rush peak. In other words, the metal, supported by central banks, will not participate in the general deflation.

But let me repeat: investors should consider only those precious metal shares which can earn enough to pay generous dividends on the basis of expected gold and silver prices. If none are available, the group should indeed be passed up.

CHAPTER 22

Why Not Swing a Little?

WHETHER IN A BULL or a bear market, every investor who can afford to should allocate a small percentage of his capital for high-potential speculating. No, I don't think anyone should waste a dime playing the market blindly. But buying those securities which, if certain developments occur, could double or triple in price should be an integral part of the Total Investment approach.

Naturally, the investor must be prepared to lose a substantial part, if not all, of the capital so employed. But as long as he understands the risk and does not use more money than he can financially and emotionally afford for this purpose, this kind of calculated speculation could enhance the overall results in the long run. It also adds a little spice to investing.

In a sense, most low-priced stocks, especially those of venture companies, can be classified as long-shot speculations. But they are not what I call High-Potential Speculations. Even with diversification, investors buying those stocks in a bear market will probably come out on the losing side—because the economic environment ahead will almost certainly be unfavorable for these companies.

By my definition, a suitable High-Potential Speculation is a situation that not only can multiply one's capital, but also has at least a 50-50 chance of working out. Once those prerequisites are met, sizeable investment profits can often be achieved—even if the anticipated favorable development never materializes.

Make no mistake about it, such situations are not easy to find. Thousands of analysts are working full time trying to find baby Xeroxes, but there just aren't that many such stocks around. Besides, by the time a baby Xerox does come to your attention, it is probably overpriced already. To the Total Investor, however, many exciting opportunities are available among "non-conventional" securities.

A few chapters ago, for example, I noted parenthetically that the bonds of most transportation companies are not suitable for conservative investment purposes in the years ahead. Airline and railroad companies are generally so heavily laden with debts that in the coming years of slowing business, the high cost of servicing debts alone could throw any number of them into bankruptcy.

But that's precisely the way many attractive High-Potential Speculations will become available.

Investors typically shun securities of bankrupt companies. In fact, when a corporation is even thought to be headed for receivership, shareholders and bondholders alike usually react by unloading immediately. Quite often, however, the emotional reaction outstrips the realities of the situation. Consequently, real bargains are created.

During the 1930's, literally millions of dollars were made by cool-headed investors who had the wisdom to buy oversold bonds of bankrupt railroads and the patience to hang on to them. For similar investors, these opportunities should become abundant as the economic contraction persists in the years ahead.

By and large, the common shares of companies going into receivership are probably worth very little. No matter how much they have already plummeted, therefore, they should be avoided.

But the senior securities of these companies are quite a different matter. The fact is, the holders of many bonds have prior claims on the bankrupt companies' assets, claims that cannot be compromised. Reorganization procedures can take years and years, to be sure. But if such bonds can be bought at no more than 25c to 30c on the dollar during the panic selling waves, the "speculator" can realize some handsome profits long before the reorganizations are completed.

The Penn Central bankruptcy offers a case in point. Immediately after the company announced in the middle of 1970 that it was going into reorganization, all securities related one way or another to the railroad system dropped sharply. They recovered somewhat in the ensuing months, but toward the end of that year, they were hit again by heavy tax-loss selling.

On December 18, 1970, the Holt Investment Advisory recommended as High-Potential Speculations two specific issues: Penn Central Co. Collateral Trust 6½'s, 1993 and New York Central Collateral Trust 6's, 1990. Both of them were listed on the New York Stock Exchange, and both were collateralized by assets worth many times the bonds' then market price of 28 and 25, respectively.

The Penn Central reorganization, it now appears, still has a long time to go before it is finally consummated. But in March 1972, The Holt Investment Advisory was already able to recommend the sale of those two bonds, at 60 and 53, more than double the original cost in both cases.

When you come right down to it, you'll notice that this kind of High-Potential Speculation really involves rather limited risks. The biggest unknown is the time factor. But if a security can be expected to at least double eventually, waiting even several years is well worth it.

Therefore, when some of the big airlines and railroads—or, for that matter, even industrial companies—go bankrupt in the years ahead, keep a keen lookout for their high-priority bonds.

Another class of High-Potential Speculations that is likely to swell is the high-asset issues. Even now, a number of stocks are selling well below their book values. As the next leg of the primary bear market proceeds, even more will fall into this category.

By itself, selling at a discount from book or asset value is not enough to make a stock an attractive speculation. Even during the bull-market heyday, equities were always available at such "bargain" levels. But if a few other prerequisites are met, many of these stocks can become big winners.

Let's first understand why some stocks selling below assets can be attractive and why some are not. Of course, depressed issues of companies that are expected to show revitalized earnings and dividends are desirable. But this applies to stocks selling at a premium over their assets as well, so it is not a relevant factor in our discussion here.

Very often, a stock sells below its asset value primarily because the management is unable to earn a satisfactory return on the company's assets. Hence the company cannot pay a dividend large enough to support a higher stock price. Unless some major positive changes take place, no improvement in the situation can be expected.

But if that company is merged into or acquired by another firm, a basic change will have taken place.

But why should another firm be interested in such a lackluster company? Again, if we put aside such considerations as potential earnings growth and compatibility of product lines and confine our discussion to the undervaluation aspect, the answer becomes obvious. It is because an enterprising company can get hold of the underpriced company's assets and make money with them.

But the fixed assets of a poorly run firm are not worth very much. Assets that can readily be converted into cash are more attractive. Put another way, companies whose stocks are selling at a discount from their liquid assets are prime acquisition candidates.

With that in mind, during the next market sinking spell, look for stocks that are selling well below net working capital per share—current assets minus *all* liabilities. Pay special attention to companies with current assets comprising more cash and equivalents than receivables and inventories. Sooner or later, they will be "discovered" by cash-conscious corporations. So here again, the speculation centers mostly on the time element.

I should add, though, that companies more than one-third owned by insiders should be excluded from this category. Often the controlling managements of such firms resist generous acquisition offers simply because they are more concerned with their own jobs than with the interests of the shareholders. And acquiring companies usually prefer not to get into proxy fights with incumbent managements in their acquisition bids.

Like reorganization situations, speculating on assets requires more than a little patience. Because of the limited risks involved, however, the waiting is often worth it. But for those who want fast action and are willing to accept the risk of total loss, option trading is the hottest game in town these days. Over one thousand options are now trading actively on the American Stock Exchange, the Chicago Board Options Exchange and other exchanges. This is a risky game; but if options are used wisely, the risk can be substantially reduced.

Basically, options come in two forms. A call option entitles the holder to buy 100 shares of a specific stock at a specific price any time during a specified period. A put option is the same in all aspects except that it entitles the holder to sell 100 shares of the common. The price at which the common can be bought or sold is called the striking price. Right now, only call options are traded on the exchanges; my discussion will therefore be limited to this group only.

Calls can be created and sold—or written—by any private investor. (One cannot double his money fast by selling call options; this operation therefore does not constitute a High-Potential Speculation. I will discuss writing options in the next chapter.) The maximum maturity of options trading on the exchanges is nine months. If the holder does not exercise his right within the prescribed time, the option expires and becomes worthless.

The intrinsic value of a call option is the current stock price minus the striking price, times 100 (because 100 shares of common are involved). Thus, an option with a striking price of 20 has a current intrinsic value of $500 when the stock sells at 25, and $200 when the stock sells at 22. Of course, if the stock sells at 20 or below, the option has no intrinsic value whatsoever.

Even with zero intrinsic value, however, most actively traded options have a market value if they have a long enough life remaining. Why? Because there are usually some speculators who are willing to bet that the common will rise during that remaining period to a point making exercise of the option profitable.

When an option sells above its intrinsic value, the excess is called the premium. This premium typically shrinks as the option's remaining life shortens and vanishes altogether at expiration time. It is often expressed as a percentage of the common's current price.

For example, let's go back to the above option, which entitles the holder to buy 100 common shares at 20. If the common is selling at 21, that call would have an intrinsic value of $100. But it may very well be selling for 4 (or $400). If so, it has a premium of 3, or roughly 14% of the common stock price. (Although a call entitles the holder to buy 100 shares, it is quoted as though only one share is involved.)

If, at expiration time, the common remains at 21, that option will expire with an intrinsic value of just $100 and the buyer will have lost $300 of the $400 cost. If the common drops to 20 or below, the entire $400 will have been lost. On the other hand, if the stock reaches 30—a gain of less than 45%—the option will have an intrinsic value of $1,000. That represents a 150% profit on the invested capital. This is where leverage comes in.

Actually, a 15% premium is about average for a six-month call if the underlying stock is normally volatile and is selling near the striking price. Thus, the stock must advanced 15% for the buyer to just break even. For the buyer to double his money, the stock must appreciate 30% in just half a year. Unless one can catch those major bear-market rallies close to the very bottom, this is a tall order to fill. For that reason, only on rare occasions do I consider selected call options to be suitable High-Potential Speculations.

Nevertheless, buying one call and selling another simultaneously—or establishing a spread position, as the professionals call it—can result in some suitable High-Potential Speculations in a bear market. Such a spread involves two options on the same underlying stock, with the same maturity date, but with different exercise prices.

Let me illustrate by using the common and the January 1976 options of Pfizer Inc. On July 2, 1975, the common closed at

32¹/₈, the option with a $30 striking price at 5⁷/₈, and the option with a $35 striking price at 3.

Let's suppose we sold one $30 option at 5⁷/₈ and bought one $35 option at 3. Since the sale generated proceeds of $587.50 while the purchase cost only $300, our account ended up with a net credit balance of $287.50. (In actual practice, it's better to trade in a much larger quantity to make it worth your while and to reduce unit commission cost.)

THE HOLT OPTION SELECTOR

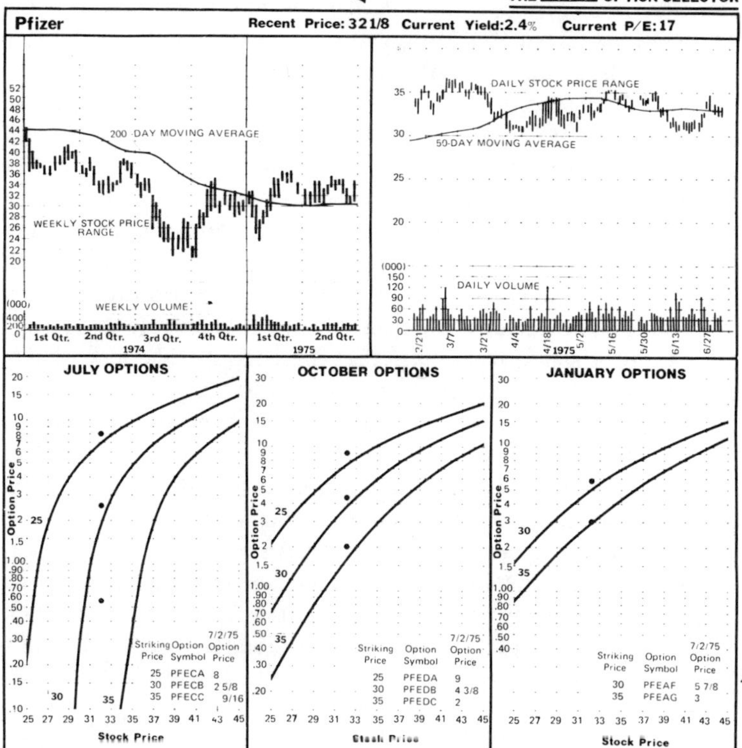

YEAR	SALES ($Mil.) 1st Qtr.	2nd Qtr.	3rd Qtr.	4th Qtr.	TOTAL	EARNINGS ($) 1st Qtr.	2nd Qtr.	3rd Qtr.	4th Qtr.	TOTAL	DIVIDENDS ($) 1st Qtr.	2nd Qtr.	3rd Qtr.	4th Qtr.	TOTAL
1972	250	264	276	303	1093	.34	.32	.39	.45	1.50	.15	.15	.16	.21	.67
1973	280	314	326	364	1284	.41	.36	.46	.51	1.74	.16	.15	.16	.22	.70
1974	353	374	388	427	1542	.54	.44	.54	.41	1.93	.19	.19	.19	.24	.79
1975	380					.48					.19				

CAPITALIZATION

DEBT: $263,900,000
COMMON: 70,155,384 Shares
PREFERRED: none

PAST NORMS

10 year Ave. Yield: 2.0%
10 year Ave. P/E: 24.3

July 4, 1975

7

Note that the striking price of the option we bought is 5 points higher than the one we sold. Thus, regardless how high the stock should go, the intrinsic value of the latter will at most be 5 points (or $500) higher than the former at expiration time. For instance, if the stock reaches 100, the $30 option would have an intrinsic value of 70 points and the $35 option would have an intrinsic value of 65 points. Thus, the maximum risk to the brokerage firm carrying our spread is also 5 points, or $500.

Since the initial transactions already yielded a credit balance of $287.50, in our account, we only have to put up $212.50 to carry our positions. That $212.50 payment represents the maximum loss to us—if the common rises to 35 or above.

But if Pfizer sells at 30 or below at the time the options expire, neither option will have any intrinsic value. Both will expire unexercised, and our spread will be automatically closed out. We then get to keep $500 in our account—the $287.50 credit that came from creating the spread and the $212.50 we put up. Note that the $287.50 profit, which is equivalent to 135% of our capital, has come from but a 6.6% drop in the common stock price—from 32 1/8 to 30. Considering that at 30, Pfizer would still yield less than 3%, I think it's safe to assume that the odds of this occurring in the continuing bear market are better than 50-50.

Whether this particular spread will indeed work out or not, I cannot foretell. But it doesn't matter. In engaging in this and other High-Potential Speculations, some substantial or even total losses will occur from time to time. For instance, among the 241 recommendations comprising the Holt Advisory's complete performance record that I presented in the first chapter, as many as three situations resulted in losses of over 75%. What is important is that by carefully picking the right situations, your total profits should in the long run far outweigh your total losses.

CHAPTER 23

And Run Scared a Little

TO COMPENSATE FOR the increased risks of high-potential speculating, the Total Investor should also engage in some low-risk situations, even if it means accepting less than exciting profit potentials. This is especially true when the market is undergoing one of those tug-of-war phases when no definitive trend can be anticipated.

An investment in selected convertible debentures may suit this purpose well. You may be interested in knowing that some years back, when these securities were among the hottest things on Wall Street, The Holt Investment Advisory specifically told investors to avoid them. Inconsistent? No. Flexible? Yes.

What is a convertible debenture? It is a hybrid between a stock and a straight bond. As a bond, a convertible debenture pays a fixed interest rate, matures on a specified date, and is senior to equities in the event of liquidation. But it can also be exchanged into the issuing company's stock at a specific price.

When these securities were heavily touted in the late 1960's, the argument went something like this: Investing in convertible debentures is a can't-lose proposition. In bad times, these issues offer bond-like protection. But being convertible into common, they also benefit from the company's good fortune in boom times. By buying these perfect securities, an expert declared then, "Anyone Can Make a Million."

Common sense knows, of course, that there is no such thing as a perfect security. In exchange for the advantages of convertibles, investors have to accept some disadvantages. Thus, convertible debentures usually pay lower interest than a straight bond of equal quality, and possess a smaller appreciation potential than the related common. Sometimes the disadvantages are more pronounced than the advantages.

Mid-1967 was one of those periods. Most convertibles then were selling far above their investment values in terms of their interest rates and quality ratings. So the advantages in their being senior securities were academic. Moreover, the stocks into which they were convertible were grossly overpriced. To make things worse, interest rates in general were expected to climb in the ensuing years. That's why the Advisory told investors to stay away from those issues in an analysis titled "Too Good to Be True."

To illustrate its point, the Advisory singled out the American Airlines 4¼'s, 1992 as a typical example of an unattractive, overpriced convertible debenture. Just issued by the airline, the bonds were convertible into the common at $47 a share through January 1, 1980. Though the stock was quoted at 41, the debentures had started trading on the New York Stock Exchange at 106.

Subsequent developments revealed that "overpriced" was an understatment. In the middle of 1975, the issue was selling below 50. The common, to be sure, had suffered an even deeper percentage drop. But losing less than the common is not quite the way "anyone can make a million."

The Advisory did stress at that time, nevertheless, that some day the positive features of convertible debentures might well overweigh the negative factors. And here's that sunny day.

Since the primary bear market got underway, not many companies have floated new convertibles. As a result, most issues now outstanding were originally offered during the bull market era. Their conversion prices are far above recent quotations of the related common stocks. For that reason, the market now assigns little value to the conversion feature and prices these debentures almost entirely on the basis of their investment value as straight bonds.

This means that the bond-like feature of convertibles now means something. A bear market for stocks can no longer depress these issues. As interest rates decline, they will appreciate in value. And if for any reason the issuing companies manage to prosper in the face of a softening economy, the conversion feature may even turn out to be a bonus.

I must point out, however, that convertible debentures are frequently issued by companies that are less than prime credit risks. As such, they are generally not good risks in a contracting economy. But with some digging, exceptions can be found.

For instance, quite a number of companies in the defense-aerospace industry have outstanding convertible bonds that are now selling at less than half their face value. Hurt in part by the Vietnam misadventure, this industry has fallen out of favor in recent years with investors as well as with Congress.

The prospects for the period ahead are brightening, though. For one thing, the group's export sales are growing, notably to the affluent Mideast nations. As noted earlier, moreover, the defense-aerospace industry will probably become one of the prime beneficiaries of mounting government spending. When the unemployment rate rises further, even liberal Senators will holler for increased defense outlays. Unless they run away in price, convertibles of these companies do represent below-average-risk, good-capital-growth vehicles. Meanwhile, many of them provide current yields of over 10%.

Writing call options is another way investors can play it safe and still make a satisfactory return on invested capital. In the last chapter, I pointed out that a typical six-month option often commands a premium equivalent to 15% of the common stock price. The premium vanishes when the option expires. In a bear market, of course, most stocks will decline. Hence, most options won't be exercised at all.

To write a single option (as differentiated from one in a spread), the investor must either own the underlying stock or deposit in his investment account an amount equivalent to 30%-40% of the common stock's market price, the amount depending on the policy of his brokerage firm. Since the chances of calls expiring unexercised are greatest when the options sold are on stocks that are expected to decline, it doesn't make much sense to own that underlying stock. The second alternative is thus more advisable. This ties up some of your capital, but if you do get to keep a good part, if not all, of that 15% premium, your profits would represent a worthwhile return on the sum invested.

Of course, your potential profits shrink as and if the stock goes up during the life of the option. But you won't begin to lose any money until the stock advances 15% or more. At that point, you can still give yourself good protection by buying the stock or buying another call option.

Hedging with warrants is still another way to engage in low-risk investing in the bear market.

A warrant is much like a call option. They are different mainly in these respects: 1) Whereas a call is created by a private investor, warrants are usually issued by the company itself; 2) while call options generally have a life of nine months or less, warrants usually mature many, many years after the original issue; and 3) whereas a call option entitles the holder to buy 100 common shares, a warrant normally entitles the holder to buy just one share, although occasionally the number is a little larger.

The intrinsic value of a warrant is the difference between the price and the current market value of the common share it entitles the owner to buy. But because warrants usually have a long life, they typically command quite a high premium. Indeed, more often than not, the premium plays the prominent role in determining a warrant's market value.

Except during major bear-market rallies, buying warrants outright when the primary trend for equity prices is downward should be avoided. Nevertheless, a low-risk situation results when a hedge position is effected by buying one or more warrants and selling the corresponding common stock.

The reason such hedges involve less than average risk is that they possess an automatic advantage inherent in the way warrants are evaluated by the market.

A look at any warrant price chart alongside that of the related stock would reveal a definite correlation between the two securities. By feeding a computer such pertinent factors as the exercise terms, the length of the warrant's remaining life, recent market trends, and the typical past relationship between the stock and its warrant, it is possible to anticipate that correlation with accuracy. Thus, for each of a selected group of actively traded warrants, the Holt Advisory regularly computes a curve showing the probable warrant prices corresponding to a range of stock prices. We call it the Presumptive Warrant Price curve.

TYPICAL PWP CURVE

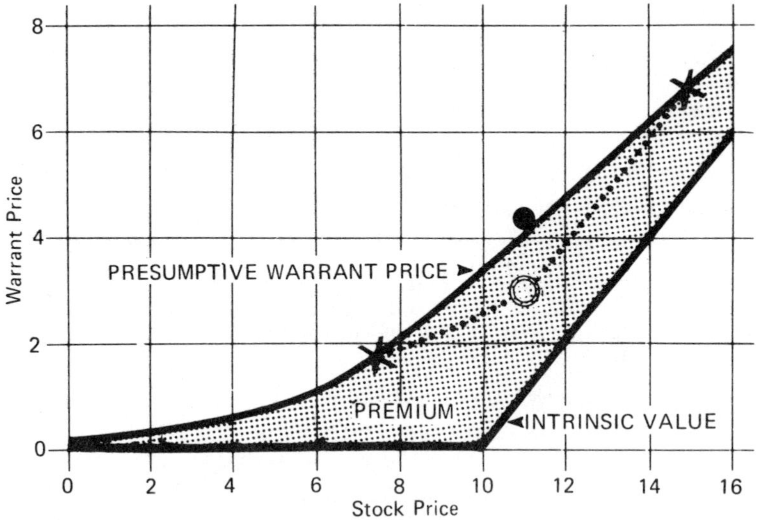

Illustrated here is a chart showing the intrinsic value and the typical PWP curve for a hypothetical warrant, exercisable at 10. The intrinsic value of the warrant is, of course, zero when the stock sells at 10 or below. But it rises point for point once the stock goes above 10. Thus, with a stock price of 14, the warrant's intrinsic value is 4.

In reality, though, the warrant price is usually quite a bit higher than the intrinsic value. Thus, even with a stock price of only 8, it may well command a market price of 2. The Presumptive Warrant Price curve is designed to reflect this more realistic relationship.

The exact slope and location of the curve is unique for every single warrant, determined as it is by the many variables peculiar to that issue. Even for the same warrant, the curve moves—usually toward the intrinsic value—with the passage of time. But the general shape of all such curves is the same.

Note that the left end of the curve is almost horizontal while the right side moves in a diagonal direction. This means that when the stock price is low, a one-point change in the stock quotation typically results in just a small fractional change in the warrant price. But the warrant rises almost point for point with the stock when the latter's quotation stands well above the exercise price.

To better illustrate this inherent advantage of a warrant hedge, let's examine the potential results of a hedge based on this hypothetical warrant. Suppose the stock sells for 11 and the warrant is 4. As the dot on the curve shows, the warrant's quotation is in line with the normal correlation between the two issues. Note that if the stock goes up 4 points to 15, the warrant can be expected to rise to 7—a gain equal to 3 points. But if the stock declines 4 points to 7, the warrant would drop to 1½, or a loss of only 2½ points. Thus, for the same amount of drop as the rise in the stock price, the corresponding decline in the warrant price is less than the rise.

The advantage of a warrant hedge would be further enhanced if, because of some temporary aberration, the warrant is available below its normal value. Using the same example again, let's now assume that the warrant is selling at 3, as represented by the circle on the chart, and that we establish a hedge position whereby one warrant is bought for each common share sold short.

Chances are, the warrant will eventually return to its normal value. If so, it will climb to 4 even without any rise in the stock price, thereby yielding a profit for the hedge. If the stock drops to 7 in a bear market, the warrant can be expected to decline to 1½. The short position would then gain 4 points, while the long position would lose only 1½ points. Result: a net gain of 2½ points.

On the other hand, little damage would result even if the stock goes up. For example, the computerized curve suggests that the warrant would rise to 7 should the stock climb to 11. In other words, both sides of the hedge would advance by 4 points.

Usually, hedging operations are not worth their while to the average investor because they require too much capital. But this is not true of warrant hedges. Under Federal Reserve Board Regulation T, Section 220.3 (d)(3), investors who own securities convertible into common with a payment of cash (as are most warrants) may short the stock without putting up additional funds. Thus, for the above sample hedge, which involves 100 warrants long and 100 common shares short, the required capital is only $300.

When the warrant price is especially low, however, it's safe to buy a few warrants for each share shorted. Even so, the total capital required would be less than paying for all transactions in full.

Admittedly, without the help of the computerized Presumptive Warrant Price curve and other leverage data, it is difficult to readily spot undervalued warrants. But the fact remains that it is an efficient capital-building tool in bear as well as bull markets. As of mid-1975, for instance, the Holt Advisory had altogether 31 such hedges. Three of them had just been established, so it was too early to tell what results they would bring. Of the remaining 28, all but three yielded a profit. And the average gain for those 28 was 27.1%. In the corresponding periods, the Dow Jones industrials declined.

Are you wondering at this point why I haven't recommended in this chapter the most apparent hedge of them all—buying undervalued stocks and selling overvalued ones simultaneously. This is just what many so-called hedge funds have been doing (and sustaining heavy losses in the process).

Simple as it sounds, this operation often comes a cropper. Why? As I explained earlier, apparently overpriced stocks have a way of climbing higher while seeming bargains often sink deeper.

I am not precluding, by any means, a portfolio that holds some stocks long and other issues short. But these divergent positions should be established on their independent merits. In a sense, such dual positions would constitute a hedge. But I regard them as merely two integral parts of a Total Investment portfolio.

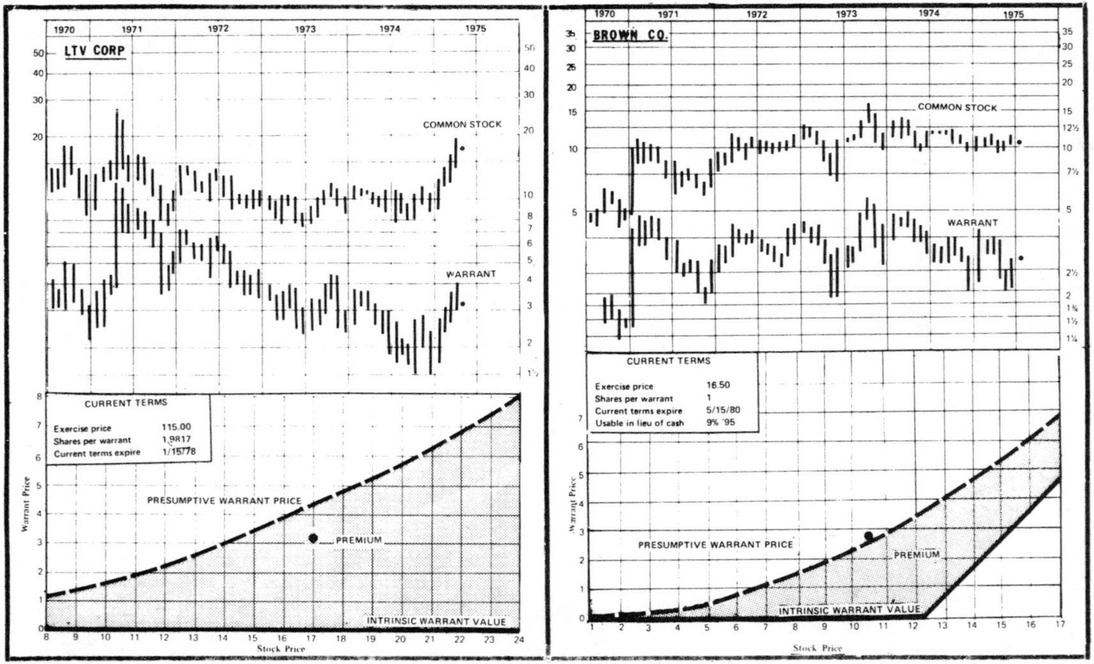

This is a sample of how The Holt Investment Advisory regularly presents the Presumptive Warrant Price curves of actively traded warrants. When the dot stands below the curve, the warrant is undervalued. When it stands above, it is overvalued.

CHAPTER 24

Negotiate from Strength

BY INTRODUCING THE Total Investment approach, I hope I have succeeded in convincing you that successful investing is not predicated on ever-rising stock prices. If a roaring bull market comes along, so much the better. But if not—and the chances are we won't see one for the rest of this decade—there is still no reason why you should forego efforts to build capital. Indeed, the worst thing to do is to sit idly by and watch your assets shrink.

Thanks in part to the securities laws enacted in the wake of the 1929-32 debacle, the stock and bond markets in the U.S. are relatively free from manipulation. In a truly competitive market, those who have superior skill and knowledge, as well as the will and incentive to succeed, will more often than not come out ahead.

Thus, if you really know the market what it has done in the past, and why; and what it will probably do in the future, and why —and proceed to build your capital on the basis of that knowledge, chances are you will be far more successful than those who invest haphazardly or those who depend on outdated thinking and discredited myths.

Some of you may be disappointed in the fact that I have not offered you any magic formula to get rich, any surefire investment for both inflation and depression. But don't expect to get such recommendations from any responsible investment advisor. The fact is, successful capital building requires much more than a simple do-it-yourself formula or an all-purpose survival plan. Time changes things—including investment opportunities.

By the same token, neither can I present you with any specific investment strategy good for all times. Nor can I recommend to you any specific security to buy or sell without knowing how it will be quoted when you read this book. But I hope I have given you something much more valuable: the realization that, with the help of logic and common sense, a flexible investment plan can be successfully implemented in any kind of market.

Let me summarize the Total Investment approach.

To start with, always remember that most of the investment techniques and theories widely practiced by conventional Wall Streeters have proved extremely costly in recent years. Actually, they never were really reliable. It's just that their uselessness had previously been masked by the post-World War II primary bull market. You would be wise to reject them altogether.

Remember too, that the views of most economists and market analysts are often distorted by political and other considerations. To analyze the economy, combine your own common sense with the judgment of those independents who have the incentive to be right.

Then, based on what economic and monetary developments are truly in prospect, estimate how much money major investing groups are likely to put into or take out of the securities markets. From the resultant Flow-of-Funds data, determine what investment climate probably is ahead.

Next, examine the major investment vehicles available and find out which are most appropriate for such a climate.

Finally, allocate your capital among those vehicles to maximize your profit potential.

Remember at all times what underlying information and assumptions you used in arriving at your investment plans. When new data become available, update your analysis and make all necessary adjustments and refinements. If a change in your investment plans is called for, make it without hesitation. Don't ever get stuck with a preconceived and unsupported position.

With the Total Investment approach, you will have a coherent investment program. Every dollar you invest will, in fact, be put to work for a specific reason. The reasons for all your investments will complement one another. Furthermore, they will all be consistent with your updated views of the economy and market.

With Total Investing, you will have that extra dimension of knowledge that should put you ahead whether the market goes up or down.

It so happens that based on current data, my analyses conclude that bond prices will trend upward and stock prices will trend downward in the years ahead. Most of my discussions in this book have therefore been tailored to anticipate such eventualities. At some point, however, new developments will occur to change the prospects. Sooner or later, the trends I now foresee for stocks and bonds will yield to other trends (though not necessarily at the same time).

Such changes will not in any way lessen the value of the Total Investment approach. If anything, they will underscore the importance of being flexible and of making use of the most suitable investment vehicles. Thus, instead of hedging with warrants, the Total Investor may consider buying warrants outright in the next bull market. Instead of shorting has-been glamours, he will accumulate reawakening blue chips.

It's not easy to be a Total Investor. It requires a lot of hard work, independent research and mental discipline. But nothing worthwhile comes easily. If you can do the necessary and the right kind of homework, you will find the research most challenging, and the subsequent rewards most gratifying. If not, find a professional advisor who can. Your investments need full-time attention.

I cannot really close this book without a few words on how to pick your brokers, if only because no one else seems to care enough to give such advice. The days of buying and putting away good stocks have long since gone. And, as you know by now, the

Total Investment approach requires periodic adjustments of one's portfolio and occasional hedge positions. All this incurs considerable commission expenses. Hence, lowering commission outlays and obtaining good service from brokers are among the ways to minimize investment risks.

Until recently, the commission Wall Street charged the average private investor was exorbitant. In abolishing fixed minimum commission rates on May 1, 1975, Wall Street—capital of the free-enterprise system—finally put free enterprise into practice. Some brokerage houses have since publicly offered hefty discounts on their commissions.

Actually, the average investor still cannot truly negotiate rates with his broker. Unlike financial institutions, most private investors are still second-class customers in the eyes of many Wall Street firms. Very few outfits are willing to deviate from published rate schedules to accommodate individual clients.

Nevertheless, free competition has forced brokerage firms to offer different rate schedules and different services. By and large, these schedules still place the greatest burden on the least active investors. But there are enough variations being offered to justify some shopping around. The fact is, private investors have far more bargaining power than they realize.

Before submitting to whatever commission rates are offered by your present broker, remember that you are in a buyers' market. The closing of many brokerage firms in recent years notwithstanding, Wall Street still has excess capacity. And while substantial now, brokerage revenues coming from institutions are almost certain to shrink in the years ahead. To survive, more and more firms will have to court the general public again. Thus, the private investor's ability to move swiftly from one firm to another represents his trump card. It should be played without hesitation, whenever necessary.

To start with, don't hesitate to ask a number of brokers to send you their rate schedules. See which firm offers you the best deal for services rendered. Then move your account to that deserving firm if your present broker is not competitive.

I should qualify that, however: if your present "account executive" has been making good money for you, by all means stay with him. Why worry about paying big commissions if you get handsome capital growth in return? Otherwise, don't let personal attachment prevent you from switching. In our free-enterprise system, no good businessman would hesitate to buy from the supplier who charges the lowest price for the same goods and services.

The phrase, "the same goods and services," is significant. By itself, the commission rate level is of minor importance. Like buying "cheap" products, doing business with a broker who charges low commission rates could turn out to be costly in the long run. The fee must be judged in conjunction with the services you'll get and the financial condition of the firm you are dealing with.

As a rule, most major firms are full-service companies. Besides buying and selling stocks, they typically provide such customer services as portfolio analysis, security recommendations, research reports. They trade commodity futures, maintain block positions, carry margin accounts, hold clients' securities for safekeeping, collect dividends and interest, underwrite new issues, manage discretionary accounts, and invest in foreign securities.

Chances are you don't use all those services. Few clients do. That, however, may be balanced by the fact that these major firms are more often than not reputable and financially strong. But if you have no use for most of the services offered, you can probably get a better deal from brokers with less overhead. Why pay for services you don't need?

Besides the commission rate, of course, you should also take into consideration the competitiveness of your broker in other important areas.

For instance, if you maintain a margin account, find out what interest that firm charges on your debit balance and what it pays on your credit balance. Determine also whether you can carry your positions by putting up just the minimum margin required by Federal Reserve Board regulations, especially in the case of hedge operations, or whether you have to ante up a whole lot more.

If you do plan to engage in short selling, ascertain that the brokerage firm can readily lend you all the stocks you want to short, and that it won't demand premature delivery on your part. When you wish to withdraw money or stocks from your account, make sure your broker doesn't take a year and a day to make delivery.

How efficiently your firm executes orders is another important point to observe, especially when a relatively large number of shares is involved. Very often, some brokers just rush into the market to complete the transaction (and nail down the commissions), temporarily distorting the stock's price at your expense. More responsible brokers would handle the order judiciously.

If you typically obtain investment ideas from sources other than your broker; if you do not borrow from your broker; and if you do not leave your holdings in your account, it really makes sense for you to consider dealing with a specialty firm. Its commission rates are probably much lower than those charged by the major, full-service companies. Remember, though, if you want reduced commissions you will get limited service. But if you are a do-it-yourselfer, why pay the extra fee? Sometimes, it's even worth your while to have a bank hold your cash and securities. The commissions you save may be enough to more than pay for the custodial fees.

One thing you must check carefully, though, is the financial health of the discount outfits. Such firms are usually small; some of them are mere two- or three-man operations. But a company's size may be quite different from its financial condition. A small firm with a modest capital may well be more liquid and more efficient than a huge organization with large capital. The firm's debt-to-capital ratio is a key point to watch.

To find out whether a firm is financially healthy, get its latest financial statements. Don't do business with any outfit that won't give copies. The New York Stock Exchange itself monitors the condition of member firms by watching their debt-to-capital ratio. It uses a complicated formula, however, to calculate the current value of the firm's capital. For outsiders, a rough rule to follow is to compute the ratio of total liabilities to total capital as stated, and do business only with a firm having a ratio of 4 or less. Stay away from firms that have recently sustained large operating losses.

One way to minimize the risk involved in dealing with financially marginal firms—large or small—is to follow a strict payment-against-delivery rule. After you have bought a stock, instruct the broker to deliver the shares to your bank against payment; and when you have sold some shares, give your securities to the brokerage firm only as the proceeds are paid to you. In other words, don't leave any cash or securities in your account.

Finally, although you are not in a position to negotiate a change in the published commission rate, you do have some bargaining power if your account is relatively active. Under the old fixed-commission rule, individual brokers were not permitted to provide individual customers any related investment services since it might constitute a commission rebate. But it's a fact that institutional investors used to obtain investment-related services through brokerage firms by paying "soft dollars." Under such an agreement, "X" dollars of commissions generated are worth "Y" dollars of outside services.

With negotiated rates now in effect, perhaps you too can work out an arrangement with your broker whereby a part of the commissions paid will be applied to paying for custodian services, independent money management, or subscriptions to financial magazines and investment services. Publicly, many major firms still may not want their customer's men to get into this kind of arrangement. Nevertheless, with trading volume likely to shrink in the years ahead, you'll be surprised how many brokers will become flexible to attract or maintain your active account. This is how competition works.

With that, I bid you happy Total Investing in the years ahead.